What people are say
PEACE FOR A LIFETIME

Get a grip. Sounds easy but I need a plan in place that helps me find my emotional balance. And that's what Lisa offers us. Insights and introspection take us from battle-fatigue to blessed. Our emotions are important to our well-being...thank you Lisa for a wellness plan that leads to Christ-centered peace.

Patsy Clairmont
Women of Faith speaker
Author of You Are More Than You Know

This is a book from the heart! Lisa shares not only knowledge, although she is qualified and gifted to do so, she shares herself. If you long for peace that will last a lifetime, this book will be a welcome companion on your journey.

Sheila Walsh,
author of 5 Minutes with Jesus

Don't stay stuck in fear, anxiety, sadness or despair. You are not powerless against your emotions. Learn how to use the Biblical truths in *Peace for a Lifetime* to find emotional abundance and new life!

Dr. Tim Clinton, President
American Association of Christian Counselors

Lisa Murray is a deep well of wisdom, grace and compassion for all who long to experience the life – and the peace – that is ours through Christ.

Constance Rhodes
Founder and CEO, FINDINGbalance, Inc.
Author of Life Inside the Thin Cage and The Art of Being

Author, Lisa Murray, has a gift of gently uncovering heart-wounds to encourage emotional healing. Her ultimate goal? To remind us of the One who heals abundantly so we can live victoriously and finally have what we all truly desire...*Peace for a Lifetime.*

Joanne Kraft
*Author of **Just Too Busy – Taking Your Family on a Radical Sabbatical**
and **The Mean Mom's Guide to Raising Great Kids***

If you are searching for a fresh breath of life again, this book is an important read. It is not just "about" the path but is a practical guide including exercises that lead you through the difficult places to authenticity and emotional abundance. This book will help you become more centered, peaceful, relational, and brave. It is in the process that we become. As Lisa says, "Life doesn't change – we change."

Bill Lokey, MA, LSPE
Chief Clinical Officer at Onsite Workshops
(as featured on Dr. Phil)

Peace is a bi-word that everyone wants but very few know how to possess. Lisa Murray, in her new book, *Peace for a Lifetime*, gives a real roadmap to any individual desiring to find peace not only "within" but also "without" oneself. This is one of those books that brings deep contemplation and freedom as you read it. It's the kind of book that will cause you to become lost under the shade of a tree as you explore your own inner *Peace for a Lifetime*.

Michael B. Knight, D.S.L., B.C.C
President - The Never Before Project
Founding Pastor - Covenant Community Church – Madisonville, KY

I have watched Lisa Murray help countless people over the years...hurting people with every kind of difficulty. Her new book, *Peace For a Lifetime*, is filled with inspiration, hope, and practical solutions for people wanting the life of freedom, abundance, and peace God has promised. Everyone who reads this book will be both blessed and encouraged!

Rick Cua Pastoral Care Pastor and Pastoral Counselor at Grace Chapel in Leiper's Fork, TN and President/CEO of Kingdom Bound Ministries in Buffalo, NY

Peace for a Lifetime will empower you to begin thriving in your relationships with yourself, others and God through hopeful and practical insights and principles. This books guides the reader through a process of reflection and then provides the tools for action! I will certainly be recommending this book to my clients and colleagues.

Amy Alexander, Licensed Marriage and Family Therapist AAMFT Approved Supervisor Co-Founder and Executive Director of The Refuge Center for Counseling

In *Peace For a Lifetime*, Lisa Murray writes from a place of compassion and expertise, offering spiritual and practical insight as she guides readers on a journey toward peace. By the book's end, it is abundantly clear that peace – true peace – isn't just some place upon which you might fortuitously stumble; it is a destination of health, of hope, of life, built upon the unfailing promises of God.

Janice Gaines, Motown Gospel Recording Artist EJ Gaines, Attorney and Artist Manager

PEACE FOR A LIFETIME

PEACE FOR A LIFETIME

Embracing a Life of Hope, Wholeness &
Harmony Through Emotional Abundance

Lisa Murray

Blessings + Peace !

Lisa Murray

Psalm 29:11

Copyright page

Cover Design by Matt Dolan
Page layout by Matt Dolan
Cover Photograph by Patrick Berger

CONTENTS

We are not at peace with others
because we are not at peace with ourselves,
and we are not at peace with ourselves
because we are not at peace with God.

—Thomas Merton

ACKNOWLEDGEMENTS

My deepest gratitude to my Heavenly Father. In You I find my beginning and my ending. In You I find my salvation, my belovedness, my identity. In You I find my hope. In You I find my peace.

To my husband, my best friend, and my companion on this journey. You have taught me so much about strength, resilience, and love. You have been my respite. My encourager. My rock.

To my mother and father, Pat and Chuck Springer, whose legacy of faith and love has impacted me more than you will ever know. You two have been, quite simply, the greatest influences in my life. My love for you is a deep river: quiet, unwavering, and powerful.

To my high school English teacher, Donna Kutno. Thank you for sharing with me your love of words.

To Monica Coates for beginning this writing journey with me. For encouraging me to put one foot in front of the other, to continue writing one page after the other, even on the days I felt like quitting.

To my pastor, Steve Berger. You have been my shepherd, my teacher, my friend. You have walked with me through so many chapters and seasons of my life. You have faithfully modeled Christ to me—I am deeply grateful for your service to the body of Christ as well as your leadership in my life.

To my dear friend and colleague, Rick Cua. Thank you for your never-ending grace, encouragement, and support through this process.

To my literary agent, Wayne Hastings. Thank you for patiently coaching me each step along the way throughout this process. For offering your incredible wisdom and direction, but most importantly, for your willingness to usher me into a whole new world that I never dreamed existed and for believing that I could.

FOREWORD

Peace isn't just a word. Peace is a reality that is sorely needed in today's troubled and broken world. By peace, I don't mean something that can be experienced merely as a consequence of external circumstances lining up just perfectly. In fact, the peace we all need doesn't come from tidy circumstances, it comes from a Loving Father. Our peace comes from a Person, and my dear friend Lisa Murray does a fantastic job of leading us beside His still waters where peace that surpasses understanding flows abundantly.

For the last 20 years I've had the privilege of watching Lisa walk in peace. In three areas of life that are often turbulent at best, marriage, continuing education and career, I've had the honor of a ringside seat watching Lisa excel with peace. I watched Lisa patiently and peacefully wait for her "Knight in Shining Armor" when she could have easily and hastily settled for someone else, like so many do. She let peace and not pressure rule her actions. I've watched Lisa patiently and peacefully study, graduate and reach her goal of becoming a professional therapist. Once again, she let peace and patience guide her steps. Finally, I've watched Lisa peacefully build her career as she has developed a thriving practice and ministry where hurting, confused, and tormented people have found peace and healing through her gentle voice and biblical wisdom. What I'm saying is, Lisa has written a book that she has first *lived* and then published. Friend, Lisa is an experienced guide who takes nervous trekkers to higher heights of understanding and freedom that results in peace of mind and spirit. Journey with her, you'll be thrilled that you did.

Peace for a Lifetime will educate and empower you with tested principals that produce tangible results. I heartily invite you to personally walk through the pages of this book where you will come face to face with the Prince of Peace. When that happens you'll discover hope, wholeness and harmony through the emotional abundance He so freely gives. God bless you mightily, shalom!

Pastor Steve Berger
Grace Chapel, Franklin, Tn.

INTRODUCTION

Peace is the only battle worth waging.[1]
—Albert Camus

Peace. Everybody wants peace. Nations protest for peace. Individuals cry out for peace. Peace is quite possibly the single greatest global pursuit. There are many kinds of peace we seek: spiritual peace, national peace, economic peace, peace within our homes, and peace within ourselves. Despite all of the energy spent in pursuit of this one thing, it seems strange that so few people ever discover true and lasting peace.

We tell ourselves that we would be at peace if we lost thirty pounds, if we had another job, if our spouse loved us more. We spend billions of dollars each year on countless books, diets, and quick-fixes to assist us in our pursuit of peace. We believe if we achieve our goals, then our lives will be better, we will be happy—we will be at peace.

In truth, while there are many amazing resources and worthwhile programs that can help inspire and motivate us to achieve whatever goals we might have, if we don't have an accurate understanding of our individual make-up, then we are simply treating the symptoms of our problem instead of treating the underlying problem itself.

---

1 Albert Camus, "After Hiroshima: Between Hell and Reason," *Combat,* Aug. 8, 1945.

We are Multi-Dimensional Beings

Human beings are multi-dimensional beings. God created us as physical, spiritual, *and* emotional beings. These aspects are, in essence, three legs of the stool that makes up the whole being. If we put all of our energies into building a strong physical being, yet ignore our spiritual and emotional beings, our stool cannot stand, cannot provide stability, and will ultimately collapse.

In the same way, focusing on the physical and spiritual dimensions of life will increase our overall health, but two legs of a stool aren't much better than one if the object of the stool is to stand. A two-legged stool is still destined for weakness and collapse.

The one consistently ignored aspect of our being is our emotional self. Yet our emotional health is fundamentally important to the overall functioning and stability of our lives. If we want to be strong, if we want to experience stability and peace, the emotional area of our lives must be acknowledged and pursued.

Spiritual/Emotional Reciprocity

We will only be as spiritually healthy as we are emotionally healthy, yet most of us have never been properly equipped to recognize and pursue emotional abundance. In reality, many of us have been taught emotions are bad, that showing any emotion is weakness. Some of us are afraid of our emotions. We live, therefore, a life on the surface. We graduate from high school and either go to college or get a job. We find someone to marry and we have children. We struggle to pay the bills and to save for retirement. All along, we merely survive the weeks waiting for the next Friday to come when we will be freed once again from the monotony of our existence.

There are some who recognize there is more to life and work, and strive to find meaning beyond that surface existence. Many people have a powerful encounter with God and pursue spiritual growth. They study the Scriptures, join Bible studies, head committees, chair church boards, and become well-versed in *Christianese*—the language used in Christian culture to express or define spiritual concepts. They work hard to develop spiritual peace, but too often these same people use their spiritual intelligence to protect themselves from ever acknowledging or dealing with their emotional wounds. They become the *walking wounded.*

We know these people. We've encountered them and perhaps we've felt the sting of their defenses. Maybe that person is staring back at us from the mirror.

My Life as the Walking Wounded

This was my story. From childhood, I was an achiever. I studied hard in school, excelled in music, regularly volunteered in the community. I won a scholarship to an esteemed college and had everything I was told would give me peace. Still, nothing did give me peace.

I grew up in church. I was the VBS memory-verse champion and the lead in many musical productions. By sixth grade, I could recite the books of the Bible forward and backward from memory. I was an active member with Girls in Action, in youth groups, and regularly sang on the worship team. I even spent eight years in my early twenties participating in the Bible Study Fellowship program. I knew the Word. I believed the Word. But for some reason, when I heard the message preached on Sunday, there was always a deep ache inside me. I felt the life my pastor was talking about must be for others. Somehow that life wasn't for me.

Over the years, as I've counseled thousands of men, women, and families in my therapeutic practice, I've discovered my childhood experience was not so uncommon. Many of us go to church and have a spiritual awakening. We find peace with God, strengthening our spiritual self, but in the process, no matter how much we read the Bible and pray, we simply cannot find freedom from our emotional wounds.

As I gained the courage to look at the emotional area of my life, I began to find healing and wholeness. Along that journey, my relationship with God became the source and foundation for my emotional healing, and the stronger I became emotionally, the stronger I became spiritually. For the first time in my life, all the areas of my life–physical, spiritual, and emotional–were connected. Their connection allowed me to know God in deeper and more profound ways. Their unity allowed me to know and to experience myself in a meaningful way, and, finally, freed me to experience others in a healthy, loving way.

What if those of us in the church could not only be the spiritual hospital for the world in need of Christ, but also could become the emotional hospital where people could safely acknowledge their emotional wounds and find God's healing? We would no longer be the *walking wounded*. We would not only find healing, but we would also be whole.

I often wonder what kind of impact that could have on the world around us? What would first understanding our anger and then healing from our anger be like, so we no longer destroyed our families? What would happen if we were able to get the love we need from ourselves and God so we were not compelled to search for love in every relationship or sexual encounter? What if we were able to find the peace we so desperately long for by discovering and dealing with our emotions instead of numbing and distracting ourselves from them with the next drink, the next big deal at work, or the next binge and purge?

Peace is the essence and purpose of this book. Peace doesn't have to be an elusive dream. Peace can be cultivated and nurtured in our lives and relationships.

There is so much hope. We can heal. We can learn. We can grow. In John 10:10 (NKJV) Jesus shares, *I have come that they may have life, and that they may have it more abundantly.* Why should we settle for less than complete healing and emotional abundance when that's precisely what He desires for us?

That power for healing lies within the church body. When we commit to being whole spiritually, physically, *and* emotionally, we can empower a new generation to truly make a difference in our families, our communities, and even our nations. Come with me as we set off on our journey toward peace. Give yourself the gift of taking this season of your life to discover and claim the abundance God has for you. The rewards you receive will be well worth the effort!

Chapter One

The Journey Toward Abundance

*...and then the day came when the risk to remain tight, in a bud,
became more painful than the risk it took to blossom...[2]*

—Elizabeth Appell

Discovering Emotional Abundance

I watched as the light changed from red to green. Cautiously,
I pressed the gas pedal and accelerated through the intersection
of this quaint little town. I had been through this intersection so
many times before, but never to this destination.

The building was once a historic home, now turned into offices.
As I entered the office, the corner office in the front of the house,
I noticed two large windows. Old windows—windows where the
glass slightly distorts the images outside, almost like a watercolor
painting.

---

2 Elizabeth Appell, "Risk," 1979.

In between the two windows was a large fireplace. Though the fireplace did not work, and there was no fire lit, I immediately felt its warmth, as if something told me I was safe here.

I moved toward the sofa and noticed a book displayed on the mantel of the fireplace—one book sitting alone. *The book must be important*, I thought. I didn't know how important.

That day, my first day, was the beginning of my healing. I had arrived here after a season I like to call the *season of my undoing*. Like those in recovery say, life had indeed become unmanageable.

No, there was no addiction, no rehab, or such. That might be easier to label somehow. I had simply come to the end of myself, and I could go no farther. I had reached, for me, the place of critical mass.

Change was no longer a matter of choice. Change was a necessity.

Like everything else in life, change was a process, so he said. My therapist spoke eloquently of a journey. He said since I didn't arrive here overnight, I probably would not get out of here over-night. He said to trust the process. I did. I had no other choice.

Week after week, I would stare out the windows—those big, old windows—as we talked. In the fall, I watched the wind bluster through, causing the trees to shed their leaves. I watched the barren winter wield its mighty hand, reducing nature to a cav-ernous nothingness. I watched as the spring came and the leaves, the bright yellow-green leaves, began to paint their watercolor brilliance once again.

One day as I peered outside, I could see the wind gently blow-ing through the branches of those old ancient trees. Like waves on the seashore, theirs was a gentle ebb and flow, as if life was being breathed back into them. I felt life begin to breathe inside of me, too.

As my eyes scanned the room, my glance caught the outline of the book, that lone book on the mantel. I began to study the book. The title, *Abba's Child*[3], months ago at my first visit here, made me angry. I didn't feel like Abba's child. Over time, my anger gradually shifted to sadness, then curiosity, then longing.

He never mentioned the book. The book was simply sitting there, waiting until I was ready. One day, I was ready.

The book, which held tremendous importance to me, was the beginning of something larger, something seismic. The book began to open a whole new world to me, a world of new understanding. A new understanding of emotions. Of wounds. Of healing and wholeness. Of identity. Of peace.

I recall pondering over and over again, *How is it I have never heard of this before? Why has no one ever told me there was emotional healing available to tend my wounds? Why do they not teach about emotional health to every child in school?*

My journey propelled me from therapy to graduate school. I could not get enough. My quest wasn't just about health, but also about emotional *abundance*. The language they spoke was a language I understood. This language made sense in a way so much in my heart and mind had never before made sense.

So what is this thing called *Emotional Abundance*? "How do I know if I have it?" "Are there blood tests they can do to check for it at my next doctor's visit?"

Well—not exactly.

Yet there are practical life steps that can be cultivated in our lives that will increase our level of Emotional Abundance (EA). For each step we take toward EA, we take one step away from the

---

3 Brennan Manning, *Abba's Child* (Colorado Springs, CO: NavPress, 1994).

anxiety and chaos surrounding us, or perhaps residing within us. Each step we take toward EA brings us one step closer toward stability, one step closer toward—peace.

What is Emotional Abundance?

In order to better understand the concept of Emotional Abundance, we need to break down and define each word to grasp the fullest meaning. The first word, *emotion*, comes from the French word, *emouvoir*, which means to excite. The *Oxford Pocket Dictionary of Current English* defines emotion as "an instinctive or intuitive feeling, as distinguished from reasoning or knowledge; a natural instinctive state of mind deriving from one's circumstances, mood, or relationship with others."[4]

So in a practical sense, emotions are the natural, instinctive, feeling responses we get as we come in contact with circumstances and/or relationships. Emotions are not bad. Emotions are not meant to be suppressed nor are they meant to control or dominate our attitudes and decisions.

I love this—we were created to feel. Ecclesiastes 3:1,4,8 (NKJV) describes that, *To everything there is a season, A time for every purpose under heaven … A time to weep, and a time to laugh … A time to mourn, and a time to dance … A time to love, and a time to hate; A time of war, and a time of peace.*

The second word, *abundance*, is defined in Random House Online Dictionary as "an extremely plentiful or over-sufficient quantity or supply; overflowing fullness; abundance of the heart."[5] The word *abundance* stems from the Latin *abundantia* meaning *abounding*.

4 *Oxford Pocket Dictionary of Current English,* 11th ed., s.v. "emotions."
5 *Abundance.* Dictionary.com. *Dictionary.com Unabridged.* Random House, Inc. http://dictionary.reference.com/browse/abundance (accessed: March 09, 2015).

Emotional Abundance, therefore, can be described as the over-sufficient supply, the overflowing fullness in the area of our instinctive, intuitive, feeling responses as we come in contact with our environment and our relationships. EA is the ability to feel our emotions, to reason through our emotions, to understand our emotions, and to effectively manage our emotions so we can appropriately respond to the people and circumstances around us. EA is the capacity to meet the demands of everyday life and create meaning in order to move forward in a positive direction. We can experience Emotional Abundance in our relationship with God, in our relationship with ourselves, and also in our relationships with others.

I like these definitions. EA means that I am not a helpless victim of my emotions; nor am I required to be cut-off from my emotions. I can experience abundance *in* my emotions!

The Benefits of Emotional Abundance

Some studies have shown that EQ or *Emotional Quotient* has been determined to play a more powerful role in our success (as much as 80%), while IQ (Intellectual Quotient) has been shown to determine only about 20% of success.[6] How we learn to deal with our emotions determines more about our overall success in life than the grades we got in school or the degree we earned from college.

In his book, *Emotional Intelligence*, Daniel Goleman says, "People with well-developed emotional skills are also more likely to be content and effective in their lives, mastering the habits of

---

6 John Chancellor, *http://johnchancellor.hubpages.com/hub/ Why-Emotional-Intelligence-is-More-Important-Than-IQ.*

the mind that foster their own productivity; people who cannot marshal some control over their emotional life fight battles that sabotage their ability for focused work and clear thought."[7]

Emotional Abundance also has a direct impact on our physical health. Experts agree that over eighty percent of our health problems are stress-related. When we don't know how to manage and reduce the stress in our lives, our physical health will suffer.

Our relationships are positively affected by Emotional Abundance as well. The more we are able to feel, understand, and manage our emotions, the better able we are to express them in a healthy way to the people around us. Whether at work or in our personal lives, relationships will flourish as we are able to be with and listen to another person's perspective in order to work through conflicts or disagreements.

Emotional Abundance can have a great impact on our spiritual lives. To be with, listen to, quiet ourselves with, and find meaning in our relationship with God will not only strengthen our spiritual lives, but will make our spiritual lives abound to overflowing.

Developing Independence

In perhaps the most fundamental sense, our level of Emotional Abundance is determined by our level of independence, both emotional and financial. Something happens when we leave the safety and comfort of home and go out to build our lives, to pursue our dreams, and to conquer the world. We build a sense of confidence in our competence to accomplish even the little things—being able to pay rent or being able to buy our mother a birthday present with the money we earned. That season in

---

7 Daniel Goleman, *Emotional Intelligence* (New York: Bantam Books, 1995).

my life was so exhilarating for me. I can remember struggling financially for so long, living on potatoes and ramen noodles, and finding every free activity possible to do with friends. Still, I was doing life on my own and I loved being independent. This time was part of my growing up, becoming an adult financially.

Independence doesn't just mean financial independence though. Independence needs to be developed emotionally as well. Emotional independence means that I don't rely on other people to meet my emotional needs. We know that social support is necessary, however, "people who are emotionally dependent tend to rely on getting good feelings about themselves from the outside rather than from within."[8]

Emotional independence means that I own responsibility for my emotions and therefore my life. Owning responsibility enables me to make positive changes in my life without staying stuck in anger or disappointment, or blaming others for the circumstances in my life. For me, that knowledge is powerful and freeing—to know that I am not only responsible for keeping me safe, I *can* keep myself safe.

Feeling, Reasoning, Understanding, and Managing Our Emotions

As we defined Emotional Abundance earlier, we included the ability to feel, reason, understand, and manage our emotions. Many of us have been taught for a variety of reasons, *not* to feel emotions. Boys hear over and over that *men don't cry* and, for this reason, learn to suppress all of their emotions. Girls, too, have

---

8 Rheyanne Weaver, *"5 Emotional Health Benefits of Being Independent."* Empowher.com, 2014.

been socialized to believe that being a *good girl* means we are never upset, always pleasing, always happy. In certain religious circles, the philosophy has been adopted in which the belief God created only positive emotions is espoused. All negative emotions must be bad, a lack of faith or spiritual maturity, an attack from the enemy, to be prayed over, delivered, or removed at all cost.

Though I tried so hard to be a good girl and suppress all of my emotions, my attempts were in vain. Instead, at the other extreme, I was entirely consumed with emotion. My mom always told me because I was a creative soul, I felt things very deeply—too deeply perhaps. My emotions were never welcomed though; they were, for all the reasons I mentioned, to be kept far away. I ran from them, attempted to keep the door shut tightly on them. I shamed them.

Allowing ourselves to *feel* our emotions is a great gift in that all of the energy we spend in *not* feeling them can be focused on reasoning through them so we can understand them and manage them well. Instead of our emotions being a tidal wave crashing in on our lives, they become the gentle ebb and flow we can actually experience and enjoy.

Individuals with EA learn how to reason and understand their thoughts and their feelings. They feel hungry, so instead of raiding the refrigerator or driving to the nearest fast food restaurant, they think through their last meal. When did they eat? What did they eat? Do they really need a snack or just a glass of water? They feel anxious, but, instead of reaching for the vodka, they stop to think through their anxiety.

Rather than allowing their emotions and impulses to manage them, Emotionally Abundant individuals are empowered to manage their emotions and impulses. Healthy adults allow themselves to experience their emotions, yet they do not immediately react to them. They are able to process through their emotions to arrive at thoughtful, meaningful responses.

One of the most important indicators of Emotional Abundance is the ability to delay gratification. This can be hard to find in our culture of *I see it, I want it, I want it now,* yet being able to delay gratification is a top predictor of success. People who are able to pay the price today and delay rewards for their efforts are going to make healthy choices physically, emotionally, financially, relationally, and spiritually.

The Power of Differentiation

Perhaps the richest component of Emotional Abundance is known as differentiation. Murray Bowen, a psychiatrist and pioneer in the field of family systems therapy, described the term *differentiation* as the capacity of a person to manage his or her emotions, thinking, individuality, and connections to others. In essence, differentiation is the ability to hold onto who we are while we are in relationship with others—being able to stay an *I* in the context of a *we,* being able to respect differences without forcing anyone to abandon themselves to be with the other.

This is by far the most complex component of EA to define and understand, but I believe differentiation also holds the greatest potential for individual peace, contentment, and joy. Differentiation forces us to look within *ourselves* to find the source of our unhappiness instead of blaming others for our unhappiness.

Emotional Abundance is a lifelong journey that is both challenging and beautiful, yielding stability and peace. Because we have focused our energy on improving the aspects of life that are within our control, we no longer need to focus that energy on fixing or changing those around us.

The questions then become these: "Can I free the ones I love to be who they are on their own journeys?" "Can I allow them to grow at a different pace and in different ways than I grow?" "Can I free them to discover and live out their unique identities, their values and beliefs, their passions and purposes?" "Can I choose to walk beside them in a healthy, loving way?"

Happiness vs. Peace

"Beyond happiness and unhappiness there is a peace...Happiness depends on conditions being perceived; inner peace does not."[9]
—Eckhart Tolle

I used to talk with my stepsons a lot about happiness. I would hear parents telling their children they just wanted them to be *happy,* and while I understand the sentiment, I was saddened. "You see," I would explain to them, "if you make your goal in life to pursue happiness above all, then the pursuit will take you to many difficult places. You will expend a great amount of energy chasing after happiness, and just when you think you have a grasp of what being happy is, happiness will disappear like a vapor before your very eyes." The reason is happiness is a feeling, one that comes and goes with equal speed. Happiness is not something on which to build a life.

If your aim is to pursue peace—inner peace—that is something you can control. You can nurture peace; you can cultivate peace in both calm and difficult seasons. Psalm 29:11 (NIV) states,

---

9 Eckhart Tolle, *The Power of Now* (Novato, CA: New World Library, 1999), 147.

The LORD gives strength to his people; the LORD blesses his people with peace.

Peace is not a feeling—peace is a way of life. Peace endures. Peace is something on which you can build a life. And the most peace-filled, emotionally-abundant individuals I know just so happen to be the happiest people I know as well.

Chapter Two

THE UNIVERSAL WOUND

The tragedy of life is not death,
but what we let die inside of us while we live.[10]
—Norman Cousins

If children develop emotionally as they do physically and intellectually, why are there so few emotionally-healthy adults? What happens that stops or prevents children from attaining Emotional Abundance – that ability to feel, reason through, understand, and effectively manage emotions – as they arrive at adulthood? The short answer is this: life happens.

We are born as blank slates. However, since we live in a broken world, that brokenness makes its mark on the slate of our identities in many ways. Brokenness changes everything about how we see the world, how we see ourselves, and how we see relationships. Life in a broken world creates broken people, and that brokenness is our universal wound. No one escapes being broken. No one is

---

10 Gurmit Singh, *History of Sikh Struggles*, (Columbia, MO: South Asia Books, 1989), 191.

exempt. Brokenness is simply the reality of life and relationships on this side of heaven.

For example, many children living in environments where they are helpless to protect themselves or those around them learn to see themselves in adulthood as powerless to affect change in any area of their lives. They sometimes begin to experience themselves as deserving of the abuse they attract in relationships, and they may begin to feel a certain comfort in unhealthy environments and relationships because that unhealthiness seems familiar. Because they feel powerless to affect any change in their worlds, they continue in the pattern written on their physical, cognitive, and emotional slate many years earlier in childhood.

Big-T Traumas

Most of us find the identification of how *Big-T* traumas can profoundly impact the emotional development of a child relatively easy. Big-T traumas are significant events like the loss of a parent, exposure to a natural disaster, or crisis situations that can arrest a person's emotional development. Big-T traumas may leave them with the *fight or flight* symptoms that can be common in those with Post Traumatic Stress Disorder. Fight or flight responses are the unconscious emotional stress reactors triggered by an event in the present that links an individual to a trauma from the past. When triggered, some individuals will react to a perceived threat with aggressive behaviors while others will react by fleeing or avoiding the threat altogether.

My friend, Jenny, a 45-year-old woman, was struck by an eighteen-wheeler while she was driving down the interstate. Though she survived without any significant injury, Jenny found driving incredibly difficult for months afterward. If she came upon a commercial vehicle at an intersection, she would begin to panic. All she could see was the truck coming through the light and crashing into her car. Her heart would begin to race, and she would feel light-headed and dizzy. She would become paralyzed and could not move her vehicle for several minutes after the other vehicle passed. Until treated, this Big-T trauma was debilitating.

Judith Herman, the author of *Trauma and Recovery*, writes, "after a traumatic experience, the human system of self-preservation seems to go into permanent alert, as if the danger might return any moment."[11] Because children don't have the cognitive or emotional capacity to process these traumas, they may develop defense mechanisms and coping strategies. Such strategies help them feel a measure of control in a world where they feel quite helpless and out of control.

Kevin was thirty-two years old when he and his wife, Stacy, twenty-eight, came to see me for their first counseling session. They had been married for six years, but they were on the verge of divorce because of Stacy's control issues. Kevin alleged Stacy controlled everything in their marriage, including the finances, household chores, and parenting of their three- and five-year-old girls. Stacy decided what and when they ate, what movies they saw, their activities, and their friends. If everything went according to Stacy's plan, the family could enjoy a pleasant afternoon. But if something didn't fall into place perfectly, Stacy usually became agitated, critical, and often enraged at Kevin or the girls. Whenever Kevin wanted to offer his opinion or make a suggestion, he was ignored, belittled, or threatened. Those experiences left Kevin

---

11 Judith Herman, *Trauma and Recovery* (New York: Basic Book, 1997), 35.

feeling resentful and bitter toward Stacy.

During their initial visit, I discovered that Stacy's mother had been brutally murdered when she was twelve years old. After the loss, she was taken to a counselor once, but shortly after that, her father remarried and moved the family several states away. Since she wasn't getting into trouble and appeared to be doing okay, her father didn't see the need to continue her counseling sessions.

In therapy, Stacy revealed she began having terrible nightmares of something happening to her after her mother's death, or, even worse, to her father. He was all she had left. If something happened to him, what would she do? Who would look after her?

She began pulling her hair out several months later, a habit she was continuing at the time of our sessions. Her anxiety was at an extremely high level and was accompanied by severe periods of depression.

Stacy is an example of how a Big-T trauma during childhood can dramatically impact how we function in relationships as adults. However, Big-T traumas are not always from exposure to a single traumatic event. Big-T traumas may also result from sustained exposure to significant physical or emotional neglect or abuse over a long period, or repeated incidents of sexual abuse or sexual molestation. Big-T traumas can occur if we are loaded with an overwhelming amount of *emotional baggage* in childhood. Should there be no one to help us unpack and detach from those situations, we are left to carry this baggage with us into our adult life, our jobs, our marriages, and our relationships with our children.

Jack was fifty-two years old when he sought treatment for depression after an attempted suicide. In our initial session, Jack revealed his mother had been diagnosed with Bipolar Disorder and Borderline Personality Disorder. Consequently, he and his sister felt as if they had to walk on eggshells for their entire childhoods. They never knew what might cause another terrible rage in which their mother would become verbally, emotionally, and physically abusive toward them.

Jack's father was an object of his mother's abuse too; however, his father was fairly passive and did little to protect the children from her explosions. Jack's mother repeatedly told him he wasn't going to amount to anything, he was a loser, and he was the *stupid one in the family*.

Though today Jack can recognize his mother was mentally ill, he still finds holding a steady job difficult, and he has two failed marriages. In addition, his children have drained him financially and emotionally because he has trouble denying their repeated requests for money.

While Stacy and Jack may represent extreme examples, the unfortunate reality is millions of individuals deal with issues like these every day of their lives, struggling to overcome the long-term effects of Big-T traumas.

Small-t Traumas

Even if we have never experienced that level of trauma, we all have experienced smaller traumas over the course of our childhoods, which have yielded tremendous wounds. Those wounds impact every circumstance, every job, and every relationship. Such *small-t* traumas are the seemingly insignificant events or dynamics present within our families of origin (the families that raised us), which imprint themselves on us as children. Small-t traumas alter the way we experience both ourselves and others.

Some small-t traumas might include being picked on in class (not the kind of persistent bullying that over time could fall into the category of a Big-T trauma), always being criticized by a parent, or even facing the ridicule or rejection from friends. Small-t traumas are unavoidable. No parent can entirely protect their children from those experiences. They happen just as life happens. Unfortunately, every child experiences those emotional injuries against the fragile backdrop of who they are or who they see themselves to be. Over the years, more weights are added until we arrive at adulthood with a bag full of them. Some of those weights are heavier than others, some more painful than others, but all of them are powerful in determining how we experience ourselves, our relationship with God, and our relationships with others.

Family Dynamics

While Big-T and small-t traumas may have a profound impact on a child's emotional development, the influence the family system as a whole exerts upon us in childhood can be equally profound, shaping our adult lives and relationships in many ways. Families each have a unique dynamic for how they deal with the anxieties of life and how they deal with the anxieties in their relationships. That dynamic gets passed down from one generation to the next. Though that dynamic may never be articulated or verbalized, every member of the family unconsciously feels and is influenced by those subtle currents. As with the ocean, the deep currents may be difficult to see on the surface, yet the undertow can be powerful enough to influence our movements and position in the water.

We learn from our parents as we watch them interact in their relationship with each other. Those lessons later influence how we interact in our adult relationships. As families develop ways to deal with certain anxieties, each family member adopts his own coping style. We assume certain roles in an attempt to function around that familial anxiety so we can maintain some equilibrium within the family. We then carry that dynamic and coping style into our adult family and relationships.

Debra, a forty-eight-year-old single woman, entered therapy to deal with her addiction to alcohol. She soon revealed that her father was an alcoholic who was extremely abusive to her mother. As the oldest child, Debra began to assume the role of *protector* for her mother against the drunken blows from her father.

Now, as an adult woman, Debra can reflect on most of her past relationships and see how she unconsciously put herself in situations where she became the protector in each of those relationships. Whether she had to protect her boyfriends from their ex-wives, their bosses, or their children, Debra was always there, ready to jump in and provide protection from any perceived attacks. That adopted role created a codependency within her relationships and prevented both Debra and her partners from experiencing their relationship free from the anxiety that kept them both locked into an unhealthy pattern.

My personal experience has taught me a great deal about the lasting impact of small-t traumas and family dynamics on our lives long after we leave our childhood home. I grew up in a family of four with an older brother who was a musical prodigy. As my parents nurtured my brother's talent, an increased emphasis was placed on excellence and being *special*.

My parents are wonderful people. They had an extraordinary work ethic. However, when I was six years old, I began to experience myself as someone who needed to perform well in order to be *special* and, for this reason, worthy of love. If I performed well academically, musically, or athletically, then everything was great. I could breathe more easily for another day. If I didn't perform well, I felt as if the world was caving in on me. The sense of worthlessness I felt was overwhelming.

For a long time, I was able to manage my anxiety and keep up a façade of confidence. Throughout high school and college, I felt as if I was at the top of my game. I excelled in my classes and won many vocal competitions while working multiple jobs to support myself. However, after graduation, the real world began to exert a gravitational pull on my hopes, dreams, and identity. My self-esteem began to crumble. My anxiety level skyrocketed. I began having panic attacks as the emotional stakes of each performance grew higher and higher. I started to spiral downward.

Somewhere in my mid-twenties, I came to the end of my season of undoing and began my journey to healing and wholeness. I grew to understand what Emotional Abundance looks like spiritually, emotionally, and physically. I always refer to that season as the greatest gift I ever gave myself.

For the first time, I didn't feel crazy. As my therapist began to help me unpack the events and understand the dynamic within my family of origin, all my feelings made sense. Once I could understand them, I could make decisions to do things differently than I had ever done them before. I could grow the *me* I knew I'd hidden inside. I began to experience myself as a strong, solid self, rather than a passive participant.

In addition, I could give myself permission *not* to be perfect. For the first time, I allowed myself to be gloriously imperfect and still be loved by God and myself. That freed me from needing so much from those around me – their affirmation, their validation, their approval. I was able to enjoy my relationships with others and to find peace and meaning in the experience of being *in* a relationship without needing anything *from* the relationship.

My passion is to help you connect those same dots in your life. I want to help you understand how the traumas from your past and the dynamics at work within your families of origin have shaped the way you interact within your world. You can *unhook* from the past to begin laying a different foundation for the rest of your life. The chance never comes too late. The pursuit of health will always lead us toward greater health, and the peace that results is worth the work.

God intends this healing for you. He doesn't want His army limping, wounded, unprepared, and ineffective in the fight. He wants all of His children to find spiritual and emotional healing and wholeness so we can go into our relationships, go out into this world, and impact others for Christ.

SECTION I

Peace With God

Chapter Three

FORTIFYING OUR FOUNDATION

Do you wish to be great? Then begin by being. Do you desire to construct a vast and lofty fabric? Think first about the foundations of humility. The higher your structure is to be, the deeper must be its foundation.[12]

—St. Augustine

The Necessity of a Strong Foundation

To define peace with ourselves or peace with others without first acknowledging and defining peace with God is like building an entire city on wooden pilings and somehow expecting the city not to sink. Peace with God is the foundation, the cornerstone of our entire journey toward Emotional Abundance. Remember, EA is the ability to feel our emotions, and to reason through, understand, and effectively manage our emotions, so we can appropriately respond to the people and circumstances around us. Not too long ago, we as a nation commemorated the anniversary of

---

12 Saint Augustine, *Source unknown,* 4th / 5th century AD.

the day terrorists flew planes into the sides of two buildings in New York City and into our hearts as a people. I recall that day vividly in my mind. I remember watching in horror and disbelief as the towers fell. And over the many months that followed, I remember seeing pictures of how they painstakingly removed the debris from what remained of The World Trade Center Towers.

When they finished clearing the rubble, I was overwhelmed at how big and how deep the holes were where those amazing buildings stood. I had never seen what lay beneath the street before. On my visits to New York City, I had only seen two beautiful buildings that reached hundreds of stories up to the heavens. They were architectural marvels. They embodied the spirit of a people who believe in freedom and possibility! What I didn't know was beneath the gleaming exterior was an expanse of concrete and steel, cables, wires, and circuitry experts had engineered and constructed for the sole purpose of providing adequate structure and support for everything that was to be built on top. The structure underground had to be able to bear the weight of the structure above ground.

The same is true for us as individuals. How many of us rush around busy with life, our careers, families, goals, etc., preoccupied with building our own towers? How much of our time is invested in having the *right* house, working the *right* job, driving the *right* car, sending our children to the *right* school, or being involved with the *right* circle of people? We focus our energy on making sure the exterior is polished and impressive while we devote little, if any, energy to make sure the foundation upon which everything else rests is strong and sure. What I have come to realize is you cannot have one without the other. You can't have the gleaming exterior, the lifestyle, or the status, if you haven't built your life on a strong foundation – at least you won't have them for long.

The recession in the U.S. economy over the last several years has revealed to us that the opulence of the '80s and '90s in many ways wasn't real, but was a façade. And that façade looked so good! Everyone had so much – lavish homes, vacations, boats, cars, jewels, etc. – we seemingly thought we were living out an episode of *Lifestyles of the Rich and Famous.*

Popular television shows today proudly promote lifestyles of excess – far removed from any reality I've ever known or experienced. *The Real Housewives'* franchise glamorizes and glorifies women who routinely get forty-carat diamond rings, furs, and facelifts with the same cavalier attitude with which they would order a latte. Their lifestyles seem real, until three seasons later when we read the bank has foreclosed on their houses, and they had to file bankruptcy for the millions they owed creditors. We learn the Countess is no longer married to the Count, and the residents of the Newport Beach condo not only couldn't pay the rent, they hadn't even paid the down payment.

How many of us want a certain lifestyle, career, and relationship, but we don't have the down payment either? If we're honest, we're somewhere between surviving and broke. And I'm not even talking about finances.

Somewhere along the way in the last ten to twenty years, the ground beneath us as a society began to shift. We all felt the tremors. Perhaps we suspected something was awry, but very few of us were brave enough to question the foundation. Few of us were wise enough to spend time and energy focused on making our physical, financial, emotional, and spiritual foundations strong enough to bear the weight of the external structure.

I can't help but think about the motto of financial guru, Dave Ramsey. He famously admonishes his audience to, "Live like no one else now so that later you can live like no one else!"[13] His belief is if people will take a long, hard look at the financial area of their lives, and are willing to make some difficult choices today about how they spend their money, they will permanently alter their future financial trajectory and later will be in a position of financial freedom. In short, the sacrifices they are willing to make today will bring the rewards of financial peace tomorrow.

I wish we as individuals, couples, and families would have that same mindset and intensity in the emotional arena of our lives. What would happen if we could take a moment of our lives, a season, to embark on a journey of discovery and health? How much greater could our impact on the world be if we could check our emotional foundation from the bottom up and make sure the foundation on which we are building is strong and sure?

Securing Our Cornerstone

The cornerstone is the first stone set in place in the construction of the foundation of any building. All of the other stones or blocks are laid with reference to this one stone – radiating out from that starting point – and by that determining the position of the entire structure on the building lot. Since ancient times, the cornerstone has not only been inscribed with the date of building and the builder, but also frequently contained a time capsule inside with objects from the days in which the building was constructed.

The more I think about this, the more intrigued I become. With every construction project, there comes a specific point in time, a ground-breaking ceremony, where the talking and planning are

---

13 Dave Ramsey, Tired of Keeping Up with the Joneses?," *Dave Ramsey, July 24, 2012,* http://www.daveramsey.com/article/tired-of-keeping-up-with-the-joneses/lifeandmoney_debt/.

laid aside. The building is *birthed* not just with stone and mortar, but with an identity, inscribed with the initials of its creator and the date of its creation.

In much the same way, we as humans build our lives on a foundation. We will experience peace with God as we take the time to make sure our foundation is solid, strong, and **FREE** – free from structural deficiencies, free from neglect, free from clutter and debris. In order for our foundation to be strong and **FREE**, we must actively be:

FORTIFYING our Foundation
RECALIBRATING our Emotional Compass
ENCOUNTERING God in our Abyss
EMBRACING Solitude

How much time and energy we devote to **Fortifying** our foundation will ultimately determine the amount of EA we will experience within ourselves and later in our relationships. If we're laying the foundation of our emotional lives, we must begin with laying the cornerstone – the stone around which all the other stones will be laid in our emotional foundation.

As a Christian, I cannot move on to other areas unless I first stop and discover for myself who my Father and Architect is and what He did for me in putting His Son on the cross. I must stake my identity, my purpose, my everything, once and for all, on that moment of revelation – my cornerstone. Every other stone I lay in the foundation of my life will be laid in relation to that one stone, so I must take the time to make sure I've got that one right.

While preaching one Sunday, my pastor, Steve Berger, was setting the stage for a sermon on Matthew, Chapter 5, Jesus' great teaching known as the *Beatitudes*. He explained the Beatitudes, as well as the rest of the chapter, are not merely a *to-do* list of external requirements for our faith; rather they are the foundation, the identity of the Christ-follower, out of which everything else flows. He went on to suggest that we cannot move forward with anything else until we first find our soul's true point of reference in Christ.

Examining Our Time Capsules

In looking back at our example of the cornerstone, I don't want to overlook the element of the time capsule. What is the importance of including articles, coins, newspapers, etc., in a time capsule to be buried inside the cornerstone? The answer lies in one word – perspective. Those artifacts provide clues for future archeologists as to the history surrounding the building, the community, culture, and the economy of the time. Without the time capsule, the building has an identity with no context, a form with no meaning outside of itself.

Several years ago, a friend of mine was renovating a century-old house. One day, as the construction crew tore down some walls, they found a newspaper dating back to 1899. My friend was so excited because of the meaning given to the project by that discovery. In one instant, that house went from being a nameless collection of boards and rafters to being a home with a history she could touch and to which she could relate. She framed the article so the future owners of the home could enjoy the history as well.

That time capsule created perspective and meaning for the renovation much as the time capsules in our lives provide perspective and meaning for us today. What is in our time capsule? What are the stories, values, and beliefs buried in the cornerstone of our foundation?

Anchoring to Something Greater Than Ourselves

As individuals, we ***Fortify*** and strengthen our foundations as we anchor our lives, our worldview, our identity, our values, and our beliefs around something greater than ourselves. Since the beginning of time, man has used the stars, nature, and God as time capsules to orient himself in his environment. For thousands of years, astronomers looked to the heavens to orient themselves here on earth. They anchored themselves to the study of the stars in the night sky. They carefully observed the relationships between objects in the sky along with the patterns of movement that occurred within the day, the week, even the months, and years in order to identify seasons. By understanding the larger world around them, they could predict weather patterns. They could plan and adjust their lives, both as individuals and communities, not only to ensure their survival, but to give guidance, purpose, and meaning to their journey. They also left the generations and civilizations that followed many legacies in science that impact our world today.

Farmers anchor their lives and planting around the seasons and the weather patterns, helping them determine the best possibility for a plentiful harvest. *The Old Farmer's Almanac* has been used in this country since the late 1700s to offer those whose lives are centered in agriculture a map or prediction of how they should gauge the timing of their planting and harvest.

The study of philosophy developed through the centuries as a way for man to use reason in order to understand and increase his perspective of the world around him. The ancient philosophers' pursuit of knowledge and wisdom not only advanced many democratic values in life and government, but also paved the way for achievements in the fields of mathematics and science.

Faith and religion have also been used since the beginning of time as a way of understanding the nature of man within the context of the divine. Even atheists, who at their core reject any notion of God, inherently embrace or orient themselves to a belief in the *absence of* God that anchors them and gives meaning to their lives. Just as a Christian's faith and the moral tenets to which he adheres profoundly impact how he lives his life and the decisions he makes, the atheist's rejection of God and the moral tenets he derives from his belief-system impact his life and the decisions he makes equally as profoundly.

Wandering Without an Anchor

Somewhere along the way, we seem to have lost our anchors. We have become unhooked from something larger than ourselves, and we are drifting—uncertain of where we've been, of where we're going, of whom we are. When a ship is at anchor, that ship is more steady, more stable, its movements more controlled, and its energies better harnessed and disciplined. External forces such as wind and rain do little to shake the ship from its moorings or its purpose. If she slips her anchor, the ship becomes helplessly adrift. With no stability, the ship is at the mercy of nature—tossed about by the wind, left to wander aimlessly through the sea with no clear purpose or direction.

We are in many ways as a society, as a community, as a church, and as individuals as adrift as that ship. Where we lost our moorings, I'm not sure—perhaps when we eliminated prayer in the classroom, or when we began the process of removing God from every aspect of our government and our lives. What I do know is somehow, little by little, we began to slip away from a faith, a belief-system larger than ourselves to which we as a society were anchored. We didn't pay much attention at first—the changes were small, imperceptible to most. But little by little, we too have become helplessly adrift. We say a prayer before we open a session of Congress, but most of our leaders have grown cynical and corrupt. They are no longer anchored to something that teaches and inspires them to grow in and hold firm to the virtues of character and integrity.

We say a vow before God as we enter into marriage, but countless marriage vows are broken and families destroyed because we are no longer tied to something larger than ourselves. Those tenets that guide our thoughts and behaviors and teach us to value honesty, integrity, and morality have been lost. We spend endless hours and dollars on education in an attempt to teach citizenship, honesty, and character to our children, but bullying, cheating, drugs, immorality, and disrespect have all reached epidemic proportions. We have systematically removed every anchor in society that tied us to anyone or anything greater than ourselves. In our pride and arrogance, we assumed we could teach these values, instill them in our children, and live them on our own without God. What we find is we've become a society that is a ship without an anchor. We have become disconnected from *something larger* that would provide stability, identity, direction, and purpose.

In essence, we have become our own gods. We have reduced God to the god of our own reasoning and scientific deduction. We've determined for ourselves what is right in our own eyes.

When asked, many people today distinguish right and wrong by saying, "It's right if I want to do it and it's wrong if I don't want to do it."

The problem is being our own god doesn't provide a solid, trustworthy, stable foundation on which to build a life. What was right for me yesterday might not be right for me today. How can I be sure of anything, what is there I can hold onto if everything around me is changeable, uncertain, or fickle?

Strengthening Our Spiritual Identity

When we as individuals do not take the time to *Fortify* our foundations, when we are no longer anchored in our faith to something larger than ourselves, we do not have strong identities. We crave a strong identity and desperately search for one, but we look for identity in our iPhones and PlayStations, our jobs and cars, even the places we eat, shop, and exercise. When we get the latest-greatest brand or gadget, we wonder why the high we get doesn't last, why that *new thing* is never enough, why we are constantly in search of the *next big thing*? The truth is we were never meant to be fulfilled by anything other than our Heavenly Father. We were never meant to get our sense of self from anything other than the God Himself. Perhaps He knew that we, like boats without an anchor, have a tendency to drift away. Throughout the Bible, we are referred to, directly or indirectly, as sheep. And sheep, by their nature, tend to wander. Sheep need a shepherd. Boats need an anchor. We need a Savior. (Isaiah 53:6, Psalm 23:1)

Why are we surprised that people today seem to be experiencing their lives as empty, meaningless, and hopeless more than ever before? Why are we surprised that national rates of depression and anxiety are at historic levels? As individuals, what we seemingly are all desperate for, clamoring for, hoping for is an anchor to steady us, guide us, and provide the peace that humanity cries out for. In our desperation, we'll do just about anything to find and hold that anchor—that peace, if only for a moment.

Yet we search for peace in all the wrong places. We look for peace in our careers, personal finances, relationships, and belongings. Things that were not designed to give us peace, and over which we have no control, become our emotional gods. We ask them to do for us what God alone can do. When they can't fix us, fill us, calm us, or complete us, we are left feeling helpless, out of control, afraid.

A huge gap exists between the spiritual confidence we proclaim in church on Sundays as we raise our hands in praise, and the overwhelming stress and anxiety we carry on our shoulders the rest of the week. Why is this? The reason is we have connected at a spiritual level, but have not yet connected at an emotional level. Everyday, somehow, someway, life happens. There will always be stress and frustration. How we face the difficulties of life, how we deal with the stress, ultimately determines how we experience ourselves and how we experience others around us.

The Tree of Emotional Abundance

How can we hope to face life's challenges, how can we dream of finding peace in our hearts and our relationships if we have not first found peace with God? I like to envision this peace-journey as a mature, beautiful oak tree. I grew up in Florida where the oak trees are truly magnificent! There are trees hundreds of years old whose branches and leaves are so wide and so dense they form a virtual canopy. As a child, I found them delightful to climb in and play on. But the brilliance seen on the surface is nothing compared to the root system that sprawls underneath. The roots can be enormous. Cutting one of these trees down can be tremendously difficult because there are so many roots, and the roots themselves are so thick and long.

Much like the oak tree, my strength, my peace with God comes from what I don't see – that which lies beneath the surface. Deep within is where my foundation is *Fortified*, where I become planted, rooted, and anchored. These roots will provide the strength and fortitude I need for this journey. Ephesians 3:17-18 (NLT) says, *Then Christ will make his home in your hearts as you trust in him. Your roots will grow down into God's love and keep you strong. And may you have the power to understand, as all God's people should, how wide, how long, how high, and how deep his love is.*

Thelma Wells, a great woman and speaker for the *Women of Faith* conferences, used to say that a person's ministry could only reach *out* to the extent that their roots within reached *deep*. The more attention I devote to developing a healthy understanding of God and nurturing my relationship with Him, the stronger my root system and foundation becomes and the greater my understanding of myself will be.

The root system's job is to provide strength and stability to the tree as well as to feed the tree. The roots take in water and nutrients from the earth around them and transport them up into the trunk of the tree. Without a strong root system, the tree cannot survive.

The trunk is the engine-room of the tree. Life happens in the trunk. Identity is formed here. The health of the root system as well as the soil in which I am planted directly influences my identity. Only when we have a clear understanding of who God is can we begin to understand who we are and find our strength and identity at a core level.

Next, the trunk of the tree gives strength and stability to the branches. Nutrients make their way up through all of the branches and stems to the leaves. Nourished by a healthy root system, the leaves are the beauty of the tree. Likewise, our relationships are the most beautiful part of the tree. If everything is functioning properly, the leaves will be healthy and vibrant, and as they soak up nutrients from the sun, they pass them back along to the trunk and root system. Life starts from the bottom and extends upward and life at the top, re-energized and renewed, flows back down to the bottom. The bonus is the fruit the tree bears in the process.

For so long, I had the system all backward. Because I had not planted my roots in the soil of God's love and acceptance, I could not feed my inner self with those vital nutrients. Instead, I fed myself a steady diet of self-condemnation, criticism, shame, and judgment. In my efforts to get any form of nourishment, I began to drain more nutrients from my leaves than they could ever provide. I could not understand why my relationships couldn't provide the health, the strength, or the peace I desired. The answer is they were never intended to provide those things. Only God can provide the nutrients I need to enjoy EA in my life and relationships.

Once I am firmly planted and growing well, my peace with others then becomes the branches and leaves of the tree. Whether in my communication or boundaries, I can be in healthy, loving connection with others. This relationship is not based on what I may need from them, but entirely based on enjoying them for who they are and who God has created them to be. I can love and serve others gratuitously out of my passion and purpose, and out of a self-acceptance birthed from God's acceptance of me. I can do whatever God has called me to do—whether teaching, cooking, helping, giving, or praying—out of a place of emotional abundance.

Because I have focused my energies on nurturing and building my relationship with Christ and myself, my cup is emotionally full, and I am compelled internally to give the abundance out to others. When we are filled, the life and peace we possess flows freely to those around us, and the branches and leaves that grow reach far and wide, displaying God's beauty as He intended. Our lives bear much fruit, our relationships grow healthy, and, as a result, seeds are planted and nurtured in other's lives in ways we could never fully know. In the end all are strengthened, all are blessed. That is health, and that is love.

....

Stepping Stones

- How does the foundation of your emotional house look?

- How much time and attention have you given to *Fortifying* your foundation? What things have weakened or destroyed your foundation?

- What is inscribed on the cornerstone of your house? Who is the architect?

- Can you remember a specific moment when you had an encounter with God where your spiritual foundation was poured and your identity was born?

- What items in your time capsule would give future generations indications of who you were, what you believed, what your life was about?

- Reflecting back, has there been *something larger than yourself* that has helped anchor your life?

- Where have you searched for peace?

- If your emotional self is the tree described earlier, in what soil is your tree planted? Are your roots nourished by God's unfailing love, His tender mercies, and His great compassion towards you? Or are your roots planted in the soil of selfishness, lies, deception, shame, and condemnation? How has that affected your relationship with yourself and others?

Chapter Four

RECALIBRATING OUR EMOTIONAL COMPASS

Nothing ever goes away until it has taught us what we need to know.[14]

—Pema Chodron

No Pain, No Gain

Growing is a double-edged sword. The results are generally positive, but the process never occurs without some amount of struggle, effort, and pain. A few years back, I decided the time had come for me to start exercising. Now for me that was a particularly difficult decision because women in my family are not especially athletic. While I did grow up playing softball, and spent many years running wrapped in plastic wrap in order to lose weight for pageants and other competitions, most of my extra-curricular

---

14 Pema Chodran, *When Things Fall Apart: Heart Advice for Difficult Times* (Shambhala, 2000), 40.

activities as a kid involved some sort of musical training. Since college, the notion of working-out has conjured images of pain, endless repetitions, and suffering. That was not for me!

As I began to near my thirties and the realities of an aging metabolism set in, I decided that perhaps now was the time to dust off my 1980s aerobics gear and head to the gym. That my best friend was a body builder and trainer, not to mention that another sweet friend, Sheila, offered to train with me, I felt was divine providence. This is like a *two-fer*, I thought. This was perfect.

Neither Sheila nor I were fitness types. We probably had fairly similar body types and athletic skills. Nevertheless, we both showed up the first day eager to become lean and trim. We didn't know what awaited us.

Our trainer was really into this working-out thing. I thought we would have the chance to visit while we were on the treadmill, perhaps grab a coffee in between repetitions of sit-ups. I don't think that's what our trainer had in mind.

To say she took her job seriously might have been an understatement. She kept yelling, "One more set, one more set!" I have never been a quitter, and so I tried my best to push through the pain in order to finish well. By the end of our first day, Sheila and I were both exhausted. I drove home feeling sore, but exhilarated. Once I arrived home, however, things began to change. Little by little, I noticed my soreness increased. By the next day, I could no longer walk up the stairs; I could only crawl. Sitting down and standing up became monumental and excruciating tasks. There were moments I thought the pain might never end.

Over time, the pain did subside. As my muscles toned, I felt stronger, more capable. I could walk farther and faster on the treadmill. Steadily I was increasing my weights and adding repetitions. I was feeling good. My physical body was growing, and the results were worth the struggle.

I distinctly remember hearing my trainer encourage me to "lean into the pain." She would push me harder than I thought I was capable of going, not to run away from the exercise, but to press forward. What is the saying? "No pain, no gain?"

The same is true for our emotional growth as we work to cultivate peace with God. If we can lean into our emotions instead of becoming numb to them or distracting ourselves from them, we grow. If we can reason through our emotions, understand our emotions, and effectively manage our emotions, the more Emotional Abundance (EA) we build into our lives. EA enhances our ability to respond appropriately to the people and circumstances around us and to create meaning in our lives and relationships. Even as we Fortify our foundation to make sure our base is solid and strong, we must recognize that part of the growth comes through the struggle. There is a natural tension or anxiety that arises from the process.

Developing a New Understanding of Emotions

Most people today believe that all negative emotions are bad. We are supposed to feel good all of the time. If we don't, we must find a pill or remedy to remove the feeling, so we can get back to normal.

Even in the church, many see positive emotions as divine blessings and negative emotions as spiritual attacks from the enemy. We pray that God will remove, heal, deliver. We long for victory. Few of us stop to inquire about the emotions we are feeling, to lean into them so we can understand them. In doing so, we miss golden opportunities to grow, to learn, and to heal.

For many years, I felt emotions simply happened to me, that I was helpless to do anything with these emotions. I believed emotions were bad, that they were Satan's attacks over which my only hope was deliverance. When I realized that God created my emotions and experienced emotions Himself, I began to believe there might be a reason for my emotions other than to torment me. Perhaps God understood there was an area in which I needed to grow or heal. Instead of delivering me from the emotion, He wanted me to find healing *in* that emotion, so I could learn what I needed to learn and ultimately overcome.

My journey here on earth seems to be about growth. Most of my emotional growth happens in the difficult seasons of life. Growth requires friction. Growth requires resistance. Anxiety is part of the growth process. Maybe some amount of anxiety comes from the internal struggle with the unknown, the resistance that is necessary for me to grow strong.

Understanding the Importance of Anxiety

In order for us to begin *Fortifying* our foundations, we must begin to *Recalibrate* our emotional compass. We must develop a different understanding of anxiety as well as cultivate a different relationship with our distress. From a clinical perspective, anxiety is a general mood or feeling of constant worry, uneasiness, or fear about events or situations that normally wouldn't trouble us.

Anxiety is different from fear in that fear usually manifests in response to a clear threat or danger whereas anxiety arises in response to fairly innocuous situations or internal emotional conflicts. We sometimes experience fatigue or exhaustion, the inability to relax, lack of confidence, low self-esteem, fear of public places, fear of social settings, or a preoccupation with making a mistake. All of these feelings can increase our anxiety level and can result in having disturbed sleep patterns, regular nightmares, headaches, and even excessive crying.

While there are many people whose anxiety is so severe and/or debilitating they require formal diagnosis and treatment, the truth is, all human beings experience anxiety or *unpeace*, to one degree or another. In many ways, anxiety is a universal condition. In some form or fashion, at some point in our lives, we will all have to deal with this feeling of distress. Anxiety is neither good nor bad, right nor wrong. Anxiety is not a sign of sin or spiritual failure.

Anxiety is an indicator within our emotional beings, a flashing light on our journeys that can tell us several things. Anxiety can tell us there is some uncertainty anticipated in the future. Anxiety can tell us an old trauma wound has been triggered within and there are some unresolved emotional issues that need to be addressed. Anxiety can tell us that in some way we are not anchored properly, or our emotional *tree* somehow isn't getting the nourishment needed in order to thrive. Anxiety can also tell us, as emotional beings, that we are still in the process of growing. Part of our growth only comes from the internal struggle to define ourselves, to carve out our values and beliefs, and to search for the greater ideals of purpose and meaning on this journey.

While there are many who believe there is nothing more beyond the here and now, that we are born, we live, and we die, I believe there is something deeper beneath the surface. I could never be satisfied living life in the kiddie pool. There is within me something that compels me toward something more. In the process, however, there will always be some amount of anxiety I will experience as part of the struggle.

I feel as if I am peering at an object at the bottom of a pool. I may not yet be able to see this object, perhaps the truth that compels my journey, clearly. The moving layers of water between it and me distorts the shape. Sight angles are confused by the sun's light glimmering on the water. I must lay hold of the object, this truth. As I dive into the water to obtain this truth I seek, I'm not the one who challenges the truth. I'm not the one who makes truth conform to my fickle and wandering ways, or brings that reality to live in the shallow end where I have existed. No, truth instead confronts me, requires me to conform to its unchange-able, steadfast presence, and draws me into the deep. The deep is where I discover my unique identity. The deep is where I define my values and beliefs. As I wrap myself around and cling more tightly to this truth, truth molds me and changes me intrinsically, giving me hope for who I am not yet, but who I will become. Here I find purpose in the struggle and meaning for the journey.

Let's not hide out in the shallow end of life anymore. Let's not run for the rest of our lives from the anxiety that cannot kill us. Let's **Recalibrate** our emotional compass. We must understand anxiety in our lives, lean into the emotion, and understand how we feel so we can find every bit of healing and growth possible. Then we will be prepared for whatever lies ahead on the next stages of our journeys.

Stepping Stones

- What has been your general belief regarding emotions, especially negative ones?

- Do you find yourself running away from difficult emotions or do you look for ways to numb painful feelings?

- How do you deal with anxiety or stress in your life?

- As you go through your day or week, notice moments that leave you feeling anxious or stressed. Find a time or two where you can make the choice not to run, not to numb yourself or distract yourself from the emotion. Take a moment to write in a journal any observations that you noticed. Where did you feel the anxiety in your body? How long did the feeling last? Was it difficult for you to allow yourself to feel the emotion?

Chapter Five

Encountering God in Our Abyss

Our souls are not hungry for fame, comfort, wealth, or power. Our souls are hungry for meaning, for the sense that we have figured out how to live so that our lives matter, so that the world will be at least a little bit different for our having passed through it.[15]

—Harold Kushner

The Battle For Meaning

Have you ever wondered, "Who am I?" or asked yourself, "What is my purpose in life?" Why are we here and what, if anything, provides meaning to our existence on this planet? Is this all for nothing? Is there more? These questions are not only valid, but they also are an active part of our journeys toward finding peace with God and peace within ourselves. There is within us all a quiet war, an epic battle for the answers to these very questions. These

---

15 Harold Kushner, *When All You've Ever Wanted Isn't Enough: The Search for a Life That Matters* (New York: Kushner Enterprises, 1986), 18.

questions don't request an invitation. They don't sit politely by the side. They loom overhead in the routine and mundane tasks of the day. They step ever so softly over the stillness of our souls. We might not be aware of anything at all, except that somewhere what began as a tiny tremor grows into a seismic quake. We can feel the pounding in our ears and the reverberations in our chests, counting cadence, steadily louder and clearer. There comes a time when we can no longer tune out these battle drums. We must choose, we must fight to claim this territory once and for all, or surrender ourselves altogether.

The most basic of all human desires is to find meaning to life. Individuals who experience Emotional Abundance (EA) – the ability to feel and manage their emotions – are not only able to meet the demands of everyday life, but are able to create meaning in their lives and relationships. Anxiety is the tension that arises from that battle for meaning. Kierkegaard calls anxiety the "dizziness of freedom."[16] Existentialist theologian Paul Tillich characterizes this as "the state in which a being is aware of its nonbeing."[17]

The Search for Meaning

We search for meaning in our relationships, in our passions and purpose, in our values and beliefs, and in our relationship with God. For each area of our lives in which we search for meaning, there will be some amount of struggle involved in the pursuit.

Most of us find enormous meaning in our relationships. Whether family or friends, the relationships in our lives are the fundamental way in which we experience love. But relationships

16 Soren Kierkegaard, *The Concept of Anxiety* (Princeton, NJ: Princeton University Press, 1980), 61.
17 Paul Tillich, *The Courage To Be* (New Haven, CT: Yale University Press, 2000), 35.

don't just happen. There is work involved. There is always the struggle or tension involved in being understood, in knowing where we end, and the other person begins, in having healthy expectations for the other person.

We also find meaning for our lives in pursuing our passions and purposes in life. When I discover the activities, be they occupational or recreational, in which I excel and enjoy, I find a great sense of meaning, energy, and excitement in my life. As Christians, when we discover the unique calling born out of our strengths and passions, we begin to find our purpose in life and in God's kingdom as well.

The process isn't always easy; the journey isn't always smooth. Many of us are deeply aware of our passions, yet struggle to understand if, how, or when we will realize them. Even worse, we may struggle to comprehend and accept why some passions are never realized, why some doors are never opened.

The next way we find meaning is by exploring and living out our values and beliefs. When we grapple to define for ourselves what we believe and why we believe, we cherish these values because we have fought to claim them as our own – values such as compassion, love, grace, bravery, and suffering. We not only aspire to these values, but they are those that provide meaning and purpose in and of themselves to our human experience. These values are not simply handed to us, and we do not acquire them easily. We attain them only through perseverance and determination. These qualities are often developed and matured in our desert experiences.

Perhaps the deepest level of meaning or *supra-meaning* we find is a meaning that is not dependent on others, on our purpose, or even our values, but is entirely built on our relationship to God.

The fundamental relationship between an *immanent self and a transcendent Thou*, as Victor Frankl defined, is the relationship between a God who is clearly unequalled, yet who at the same time is constantly reaching towards me, longing for an intimate connection with His creation.[18]

Even at this level of meaning, there is an anxiety born of the struggle to claim our faith as our own, not simply a religious set of rules or traditions handed down from our parents, but a relationship that compels us to know what we believe and why we believe for ourselves. This relationship challenges us to live out our faith authentically in our daily lives. There are times when I don't want to be with Him. There are times when sin separates me from Him. And, yes, there are times, if I'm honest, when I wonder if He still wants me, still loves me right in the middle of my brokenness.

The Purpose of Unpeace

In all of the places we look to find meaning, at every level of our journeys we will find anxiety. Anxiety isn't meant to be avoided at all cost. Anxiety, or *unpeace* as I like to say, can be God's flashing light on the roadway of our journey, directing us toward Himself and toward the peace for which we so desperately long. We arrive at our emotional crossroad, and we must choose. We can't keep walking down the same path of avoidance. We can't continue to run away. I implore you to stop and face this pain that cannot kill you. Choose instead to learn and grow from this unsettling and seemingly barren season. Harness this energy and allow the emotion to transform who you are from the inside out.

---

18 Viktor Frankl, *The Unconscious God* (New York, NY: Simon & Schuster, 1975), 61-62.

Finding our Abyss

We will experience authentic peace and freedom, we will develop EA, only when we muster the courage to walk right up to the edge of our anxiety, our abyss, and face our emotion straight on. Henri Nouwen, one of my favorite authors, describes an abyss as "a deep hole in [our] being."[19] We can run, but we can't get around this hole. We can try to fill the abyss with many things, but the hollowness of this bottomless pit is too painful and overwhelming. The truth is nothing will fill this abyss except that which was meant to fill this gaping hole in our lives. That which will fill the abyss has always been and forever will be the person of Jesus Christ, God in human flesh, dwelling within us. This abyss is a *God-shaped hole* that drives all of us on our journey to find peace in our lives.

In a recent interview, actor Shia LeBeouf, star of the Trans-formers movies, shed some light on the emotional difficulties actors have. He shared rather poignantly, "They're all in pain. It's a profession of bottom-feeders and heartbroken people. Most actors on most days don't think they're worthy." He added, "I have no idea where this insecurity comes from, but it's a God-sized hole. If I knew it, I'd fill it and be on my way."[20]

What LeBeouf unknowingly proclaimed here is God's immutable truth. Ecclesiastes 3:11 (NIV) states, *He has also set eternity in the human heart.* God created us for relationship; He longs to have an intimate connection with us. At the same time, He understands our inclination to wander off. Our *God-shaped hole* keeps the human heart longing for something outside itself, seeking something transcendent or eternal.

---

19 Henri Nouwen, *The Inner Voice of Love* (New York, NY: Image Books, 1999).
20 Dotson Rader, "The Mixed Up Life of Shia Laboef," *Parade Magazine,* June 14, 2009, http://parade.condenast.com/130832/dotsonrader/shia-labeouf-mixed-up-life/.

St. Augustine wrote, "You have made us for yourself, and our hearts are restless till they find their rest in You."[21] Still, humanity searches to fill this hole with anything and everything except God! Sadly, too many people spend their lives looking for something other than God to fill their longing for meaning only to discover how empty and unfulfilled they remain.

King Solomon, who had all the wealth, power, and success in the world still declared all those things *vanity*, because everything he had accumulated and achieved had cost him so much in time and energy and satisfied so little. He summarized his experience by declaring, "Now all has been heard; here is the conclusion of the matter: Fear God and keep His commandments, for this is the duty of all mankind." (Ecclesiastes 12:13 NIV)

Famous mathematician and philosopher, Blaise Pascal, echoed this truth by stating, "What else does this craving, and this help-lessness, proclaim but that there was once in man a true happiness, of which all that now remains is the empty print and trace? This he tries in vain to fill with everything around him, seeking in things that are not there the help he cannot find in those that are, though none can help, since this infinite abyss can only be filled with an infinite and immutable object; in other words, by God Himself."[22]

I cannot pour enough alcohol into the depths of this *God-shaped hole* to numb the pain of the emptiness in which I am helplessly lost. I cannot run fast enough to get my adrenaline fix of sex, gambling, or thrill-seeking to escape the numbness of this stale existence called life. I can't glue together the cracks in my soul through compulsive relationships, spending, or eating to provide at

---

21 St. Augustine, *Confessions* (New York, NY: Doubleday, 1960), 43.
22 Blaise Pascal, *Pensees* (New York, NY: Penguin Books, 1966), 75.

least a few moments where I can breathe. The glue will eventually begin to pull apart, and the cracks will become even deeper and wider than they were before. Nor can I simply intellectualize my way out of this closet, trying to pretend in my self-proclaimed sophistication this hole does not exist any more than the God I cannot look at nor believe in exists.

We spend half of our time numbing ourselves and running from the pain, and the other half of our time using every rationale to pretend the pain doesn't exist. Ironically, we appear to fear the light that would save us far more than we fear the darkness of the abyss that threatens to consume us. As a result, we prevent ourselves from passionately committing to anyone or anything outside of this prison cell of our own making.

Encountering God in Our Abyss

In the movie, *Indiana Jones and the Last Crusade*, there is a scene where Indiana and his dad are running through tunnels in the mountains trying to get away from the bad guys. After a while, they reach a point where a deep chasm breaks the tunnel in the mountain. They will surely die if they turn around and go back. But there is no way they can jump across this chasm. The hole is too deep. The gap is too wide. They decide they must step out and trust that the person who created the tunnels also planned for this. They had to step out, though there was no ground beneath them, just nothingness and death. Only *after* they stepped out did the ground rise beneath them to provide the path for them to continue their journey.[23]

---

23 *Indiana Jones and the Last Crusade,* (Paramount Pictures, Lucasfilm Ltd., 1989).

We will each arrive at this same place somewhere on our journey. We will have to decide whether to turn around and go back or to take that step out into the unknown and trust that God, who created the journey, has already prepared the solution. The ground will only rise beneath us after we have taken the first step. We must take the first step.

We will find the answers to our questions, we will fill the gaping hole inside of us only as we become anchored to something larger than ourselves, only as we **Encounter** God in our abyss. Somehow the meaning in life emerges as we surrender ourselves to the "adventure of becoming who we are not yet."[24]

The apostle Paul writes in 2 Corinthians 5:14-15 (NIV) that, *For Christ's love compels us, because we are convinced that one died for all ... that those who live should no longer live for themselves but for him who died for them and was raised again.* Instead of getting our identity horizontally from our job, our spouse, our house, or anything else, we are designed to get our identity, our values, our beliefs, and our purpose vertically through a relationship with God. How freeing to recognize that we were created by Him simply to be in a relationship with Him and to get our passion from fulfilling our purpose precisely through Him. In our metaphor of the tree, we're describing becoming rooted in fertile, rich soil that allows our roots to grow strong and to spread deep and wide so our tree is healthy and our fruit glorious.

Can you recall a specific time in your life when you made the decision once and for all to acknowledge the *God-shaped* hole within and asked God to come in and fill that void that existed for so long inside of you? I implore you, if you have never done

---

24 Brennan Manning, *Abba's Child* (Colorado Springs, CO: NavPress, 1994), 156-157.

this, to take that leap of faith and commit to the very thing, the only thing that can bring the peace for which you have been searching. Take the first step in your journey to finding peace within yourself and peace in your relationships. You must first have peace with God.

If you remember walking the aisle at a youth camp a long time ago, but can't remember any details, any feelings, any difference in your life afterward, please take a moment here and now to reaffirm your commitment to God. Write the date and time at the end of the chapter as well as the thoughts and feelings surrounding this decision. As a result, you will have a point of reference, a place in time, to which you can always refer back and know beyond a shadow of a doubt Who is your Author, your Creator, your Savior, your Redeemer, your Cornerstone.

Investing in Our Faith

The second step is to begin investing ourselves in our faith. Simply wanting a relationship with God is not enough, we must invest the time and energy to understand who God is, what we believe, and why. This analysis is a fundamental step in cultivating EA and laying a strong foundation for our lives.

We can say we love something in our lives, but if we never invest any of our time or energy in learning about that thing, in under-standing the how, the what, the where, and the why that makes that thing tick, then how can we declare a love for something we do not know about, or have never experienced for ourselves?

We could believe we have a passion for sports, music, or art because we love to watch football games on Sunday, we love to listen to music, we love going to an art museum, but that is quite different from experiencing doing those things ourselves. We can appreciate those things without ever engaging in them, because *appreciation* is valuing something at a distance.

Appreciation becomes passion only when we begin to pursue that activity, to crave the activity, to breathe in the activity, to pick up the ball, to learn all of the stats, to have a knowledge of the players, and saturate ourselves with knowing more and experiencing more. We can appreciate music and enjoy the sounds as the radio plays, but appreciation moves to passion only when we engage music, study music, learn about the musicians, their influences, and interpretations. We can appreciate a Van Gogh painting at the museum, but we can only become passionate about that painting when we have taken the time to study the painter, understand his history, his techniques, and the culture of the time.

The same could be true for our relationships with our spouses or significant loved ones. When we first begin dating, and we recognize the initial attraction, we become passionate about them, we long to be with them more, to know everything there is to know about them, their family, their history, their likes and dislikes, as well as their values and beliefs, and their passion and purpose in life. We wouldn't be passionate if we weren't invested in knowing those things and experiencing them for ourselves.

We can say we are passionate about God, but until we open the Bible and begin searching the Scriptures to understand for ourselves what our faith is about and engage in building that relationship ourselves, we will never move beyond an appreciation of God. Just having an appreciation of God will never allow us to build our lives on a strong foundation that is capable of withstanding the turbulence life brings. Only passion followed by pursuit will yield the fruit of an intimate knowledge of God. Intimate knowledge of God is how we become rooted and planted in the fertile soil of truth that creates the environment for us to experience healing in our deepest broken places. Intimate relationship with God will yield a harvest of peace, not only with Him, but within ourselves and in all of our relationships.

....

Stepping Stones

- In what ways have you tried to numb or run from your abyss? What things have you used to fill the God-shaped hole inside of you?

- If you have never made a personal decision for Christ, stop right now and pray to God, asking Him to forgive your sins and to come and live inside of you. Write down the date, the time, your prayer.

- If you have made a personal decision for Christ at some point in your life, but can't recall the specifics, use this opportunity to reaffirm your faith and your commitment to Christ. Again, write down the date, the time as well as your prayer.

- Are you passionate about your relationship with God or are you stuck merely appreciating Him?

- What prevents you from becoming passionate about your relationship with God?

- How can you begin today to invest in your relationship with God?

Chapter Six

Embracing Solitude

To live a spiritual life we must first find the courage to enter the desert of our loneliness and to change it by gentle and persistent efforts into a garden of solitude.[25]

—Henri Nouwen

Finding Rest in Relationship

You might be saying to yourself right now, *Lisa, I've already done this, and it hasn't worked. I've given my life to God, I've studied the Scripture, I've given my brokenness to God and it hasn't fixed anything. I've laid my burden at the altar too many times to count, but it's right back on my shoulders as I walk out the door. Now I just feel like I'm a bad Christian because somehow this works for everyone else, but I can't get it to work for me.*

What do we do with this *abyss* then? What is there that will heal this horrific pain that keeps us stuck in this place? You see,

---

25 Henri J.M. Nouwen, *Reaching Out: The Three Movements of the Spiritual Life* (New York: Doubleday, 1986), 38.

for most of my life I knew the Scriptures, I believed Scripture – I just couldn't get that knowledge to calm the overwhelming anxiety that consumed me! I would quote Philippians 4:6-7 (NIV), *Do not be anxious about anything, but in every situation, by prayer and petition, with thanksgiving, present your requests to God. And the peace of God, which transcends all understanding, will guard your hearts and your minds in Christ Jesus.* I would feel okay for about a minute and then the terror I felt inside would come right back.

What I have come to realize is I was looking for Scripture to be the pill for my anxiety and looking for God to be my pharmacist twenty-four hours a day, seven days a week. I was using Scripture as a formula. He wanted me to use Scripture as a way to know Him and to build a relationship with Him.

God doesn't want to be reduced to a formula, nor does He want me to find my peace in a verse. He wants me to find rest in HIM! Emotional Abundance (EA) – the ability to feel and manage my emotions effectively so I can respond appropriately to others – is what allows me to grow healthy, vital relationships. Life is all about relationships. The single most important relationship I can develop that will yield a strong foundation to build my life, is my relationship with God.

The Monsters in the Closet

As a small child, I remember being afraid of the dark. I would get so scared before bed that every night I would scour the closet, search under the bed, and peer in every nook and cranny to make sure there were no monsters or ghosts hidden anywhere in my room. At bedtime, my mother would pray with me, and all would be well until she said goodnight and turned out the lights … then things would get worse.

I could see the outline of the monsters moving through the shadows as the clouds passed over the moon in the night sky. I could hear creaks in the floor, and I would stay there with my fear rising until I could take no more. Then I would run to the safety of my mother's room. I remember lying beside her bed on a blanket and thinking that as long as I could feel her hand rest on mine, I was okay, and I was safe! You see, my fear didn't need a formula; my fear needed a person.

As an adult, what I need is not a mantra, nor a theme song, to pep me up for a few moments. What I need first and foremost is a relationship, an intimate encounter with the God of the Universe, who is so intimately acquainted with me that He numbered the hairs on my head.

Perhaps as we start our journey there, we will be able to muster the courage to face the monsters in our closets. I'm not saying this is a three-quick-steps-and-you're-cured program. What I am proposing is a lifetime journey that begins with a relationship with your Heavenly Father.

I sometimes wonder what life would feel like today if I could actually feel God's hand rest on mine, quietly, simply, as I make my way through the ordinary and sometimes unbearable tasks of the day. Though I cannot tangibly feel Him, He wants me to know Him intimately and to rest in Him just the same.

Intimacy that deep may sound too scary or just too difficult. Perhaps you are pondering putting the book down and pretending this concept of Emotional Abundance doesn't exist. But it does! I encourage you to stay in here, press into the unknown, and see where this journey leads.

Stop Running

Many people unwittingly seek freedom by spending their entire lives running. They feel they could solve their problems, and would find the happiness they seek if they were somewhere other than where they are – a different job, a different relationship, or even a different state. When we run, we don't solve the problem; we are simply exchanging one unfreedom for another, one unpeace for another, again and again.

What would happen if we stopped running from place to place and relationship to relationship? How would we feel if we took all of our pain, all of our unpeace, and turned them inward, holding our wounds in the innermost place inside of us where we can sit safely with God and allow Him to heal our deepest broken places?

If we want to know true peace, if we want the foundation of our lives to be **FREE** from the cracks and clutter, we must acknowledge and willingly face the wound we want to heal, and **Embrace** Solitude as the place where our healing can begin. Until we make that commitment, we will unwittingly carry our wound with us, contaminating every relationship in our lives, even our relationship with God.

Our relationships will only be as healthy as we are. Our passion and purpose will only be as dynamic and vibrant as we are. Therefore, we must be willing to give ourselves the gift of safely coming face to face with our abyss, to acknowledge and identify the wounds we have been carrying.

Our Pilgrimage With God

As we embark on this phase of our journey, recognizing we must walk this pilgrimage alone with God is important. While family and friends can provide great support, encouragement, and wisdom during this season of healing, we must take all of the energy we expend externally on others and begin to focus that energy internally on ourselves and our walk with God.

I've spent so much time and energy over the course of my life reaching out to others with the hope or expectation that they might love me, fix me, heal me, or even need me. So many times I cried in anguish for what others could not give or fix. In my barrenness, hunger, and need, I approached those around me with an empty cup, begging them to fill my broken, empty vessel. Because of their love for me, they might try to fill me. But just at the time I thought my cup was full, I would look down to see all of the contents had escaped and once again I was empty. The cycle continued until my friends had nothing left to pour into my cup, and I felt *my* emptiness as *their* rejection of me.

The truth is our friends cannot heal our wounds; our pain is our pain, and their pain is theirs. Yes, Scripture says that as brothers we should *carry each other's burdens* (Galatians 6:2 NIV), but we only have one Healer and he is Jesus Christ. He is the One to whom we should run with our pain, our fear, our loneliness, and our desperation. He stands waiting in that place of solitude to heal us, to free us, and to strengthen us.

Only when we become still can we silence the outside world. That stillness enables us to turn down the volume on the noise that keeps us distracted and exhausted. Only in the stillness are we able to experience both God and ourselves, perhaps for the first time in our lives. Initially, the silence might be difficult, maybe even frightening, but such silence is the beginning of true healing and peace.

The Practice of Solitude

To *Embrace* Solitude, we must deliberately begin to close the doors on the things around us that distract us from this inner spiritual pilgrimage. We must intentionally create a quiet place where we can go deeper into our own hearts. Despite the hectic pace of our lives and schedules, we must carve out a time of solitude each day. I strongly recommend at least fifteen to twenty minutes daily where we allow ourselves to be absent from people so we can simply sit quietly in the presence of God. This is not a time for a structured Bible study or prayer. During this time, we are developing a powerful life-skill of learning how to quiet ourselves and experience God.

Anyone who hasn't ever committed themselves to solitude may find the exercise of quieting the mind, slowing down the breathing, and focusing on being fully present with God quite challenging. At first, countless thoughts will flood the mind – thoughts about the day, things we need to do, conversations we need to have, worries over finances, children, work, etc. Just let the thoughts drain out. Experience them, but don't hold onto any of them. The focus should be on God. Breathing should be slow and measured.

I find breathing in and out as if through a straw quite helpful. As I breathe in, I count to three, sustain the breath for three counts, and then release the breath for three counts. Once I've grown more still, I will increase breathing to a four-count or a five-count breath – the slower, the better. As the thoughts of the day spill out, our brains will become quieter, and we will begin to settle into a deeper place within ourselves, the place where our deeper wounds, insecurities, doubts, and shame reside. Even here, we should be attentive and remain fully present with God.

We must come face to face with our shame and brokenness. We must experience these emotions although everything in us may want to reach out to the very thing or person that would temporarily take them away instead.

This practice is not easy to do, but if we can allow ourselves to stay with our pain, we can own the pain, mourn our hurts, and allow God to begin to heal our wounds in the quiet place where only He and we exist.

Continue breathing deeply. Allow the emotions that threaten to overtake you to drain from you. Not becoming distracted by anything that would take us away from this moment is important. In time, if we remain still and present, we will begin to settle into an even deeper place inside – the place where God's Spirit dwells.

Solitude is the place where we can hear His voice speak of His great love for us. Solitude is the place where we become centered, rooted, and strong. We are indeed calm and safe. There is no need to be anyone other than who we are or be anywhere other than where we are. This is, as Brennan Manning describes, "A new way of being with myself, a new way of being in the world… calm, unafraid, no anxiety about what's going to happen next… loved and valued…just being together as an end in itself."[26]

In solitude, we begin to plant the roots of acceptance and healing. In solitude, we discover the greatest of all gifts – peace with God.

---

26 Brennan Manning, *Abba's Child* (Colorado Springs, CO: NavPress, 1994), 23.

Choosing Peace

So here we stand on our journey. We have come to a fork in the road. Which way will lead us to the life we want? One road we've traveled many times before. The path has become well-worn with our pain and disappointment. Yet there is another unfamiliar road. We cannot see exactly where this road leads. Which path do we choose?

Somehow here in the place of our uncertainty, our fear, and our distrust, we hear a voice that steadily and patiently whispers to us, *"Come to me, all you who are weary and burdened, and I will give you rest. Take my yoke upon you and learn from me, for I am gentle and humble in heart, and you will find rest for your souls. For my yoke is easy and my burden is light."* (Matthew 11:28-30 NIV) So we take one more step toward Him, one more step away from the fear that consumes us and one more step toward a new territory.

At first, this new place of solitude and healing feels awkward and perhaps rather foreign. There may be times when we are tempted to go back to the old country, with its old fears and old pains, because there is a seeming comfort in its familiarity. Still, the more we experience this new place, the more we will come to trust our new surroundings. Even in our failures, if we keep returning to this place, the more we will find peace there, the more this place will become our necessary and longed-for refuge.

One day we will actually feel we are not just enduring life and struggling to avoid the terrible pain that accompanies this world, but rather we are becoming firmly planted in rich soil. We are growing, we are thriving. We can feel our roots spreading deeper beneath us, steadying us from the winds that blow, strengthening us so we can live passionately and purposefully in our lives and build healthy, stable relationships. We will find the harvest here is more bountiful than anything we could have imagined. One day this will no longer be a new territory, but will be our home.

Solitude is the place where we begin this journey home. Solitude is where we become anchored to God. Solitude is the soil in which our roots can grow deeper and stronger. Solitude is the foundation for Emotional Abundance, the pathway to peace.

SECTION II

Peace Within

SECTION II

INTRODUCTION

The only journey is the journey within.[27]
—Rainer Maria Rilke

Redefining Love

I was speaking to a group of university students last year, and as my session was winding down, the moderator opened the floor for discussion. One after another, students began to describe the challenges they faced in their relationships, whether at work or home, among family and friends. They desired to have stable, healthy relationships, but they had no idea what those relationships were supposed to look like much less how to get there. Indeed, as a result of a culture that saturates us with distorted, dysfunctional images of relationships, that any of us manage to build semi-healthy relationships that don't resemble what we see on television is a wonder.

---

27 Rainer Maria Rilke (December 4, 1875 – December 29, 1926).

I had always been taught to believe that if I truly loved someone, then I should be willing to do anything for them, that I
should sacrifice myself for the ones I love. Even in church, I was
encouraged to live by the Golden Rule, *Do to others as you would
have them do to you.* (Luke 6:31 NIV) But when does our love
for others become hurtful and destructive to us? When does our
love stop being loving and become destructive to others?

The Relationship Boat

I began to describe to the students a picture of myself in a relationship as if I were in a boat that is floating in the ocean. I as an
individual am in the center of my boat. I may be in a relationship
with others, and if they are healthy relationships, they are in the
center of their boats, too. Everyone is safe, anchored in Christ,
connected with one another.

However, there are many relationships I encounter where
someone I love is not in their boat. They are treading water in
the ocean surrounding the boat. They do not realize they are
drowning, but from my position in my boat, I can see they are
drowning. The waves are crashing all around them. The wind
is blowing, and the powerful current threatens to pull them
under the water.

Because I love my family and friends, I desperately want these
people in the boat with me. I know the boat is good and strong.
The boat provides the necessary safety and security for my journey.
So I make my way to the edge of the boat in order to throw out a
life preserver. I try to lean over the edge to reach out to them, but
they are just beyond my reach. My efforts are noble and helpful,
but at the point I risk falling out of the boat myself while trying

to rescue them, I am then useful to no one and in jeopardy of drowning myself.

In order to be the most helpful to the ones I love, in order to have the greatest chance of successfully rescuing or influencing them, I must remain safely centered and stable in my boat. I must make sure I am healthy before I can ever attempt to establish a healthy connection with someone else.

Peace with Ourselves

Once we've begun our journey toward finding peace with God, the next step is to find peace with ourselves. Thousands of books have been written on how to feel good about ourselves, how to be successful, and how to have healthy relationships. However, we will find a significant link missing if we haven't first built the foundation of our own lives well. Only as we become anchored in God and find the peace that exists only through a relationship with Him can we begin to discover and create peace with ourselves.

Our original definition of Emotional Abundance stated that EA is the ability to feel our emotions, to reason through our emotions, to understand our emotions, and to effectively manage our emotions so we can appropriately respond to the people and circumstances around us. EA is the capacity to meet the demands of everyday life and create meaning, in order to move forward in a positive direction. As we saw in the diagram of the Tree of Emotional Abundance, we experience EA first in our relationship with God, secondly in our relationship with ourselves, and ultimately in our relationships with others.

Our relationships will only be as healthy as we are as individuals. Look around you. Does drama seem to follow you? Does everyone seem to want to use you? Do you find yourself being abandoned or rejected in multiple relationships in your life? Are you the one doing the abandoning or rejecting? Are you exhausted in trying to be everything for everyone while never being anything for yourself?

Usually, we are the common denominator in our relationship problems. That is difficult to acknowledge, I know, but if we can accept and digest that truth, we are one step closer to becoming emotionally abundant individuals and developing healthy, peaceful relationships with those we love.

In an earlier chapter, we discussed how life and the negative forces at work around us write on the slate of who we are as children. We all grew up in families that fell somewhere along a continuum of what is defined as *normal*. We developed certain coping skills to adapt to the family dynamic that surrounded us. Certainly, dysfunction is more severe in some families than in others, but all of us began to assemble in childhood an emotional tool belt that contained the tools we needed to deal with life. We did the best we could. We survived.

However, what began in childhood as a set of tools necessary for our adaptive functioning, or perhaps our very survival, we have carried with us into adulthood even when there is no longer any threat to our physical or emotional well-being. In short, most of the coping skills that worked for us in our childhood no longer work for us in our adult lives and relationships. Those coping skills may become defense mechanisms that can be quite destructive to us in how we relate to ourselves, as well as others.

Most of us are not aware of our defense mechanisms. Even if we are, we may find counteracting our emotional impulses when they are triggered difficult. Our reactions or responses to situations have developed over our lifetime and form fairly stable traits that do not come with an easy *on/off* switch.

Have you ever heard of the term *white-knuckling*? White-knuckling is the strain we experience when we become aware of a negative behavior that we try to change externally or resist. The addict, instead of trying to understand the underlying emotional component that serves as fuel to his addiction, simply tries to resist the urge to use. The spouse, when confronted with the possibility of divorce, promises to stop flirting or yelling, to be kinder, to keep a cleaner house, or whatever is necessary, to keep their spouse from leaving or ending the relationship.

As most of us have experienced at some point in our lives, the change in behavior from white-knuckling usually lasts about two to three weeks. Then we slowly fall back to our original default defense mechanism. Quite simply, white-knuckling doesn't work. Unless we look beneath the surface to understand the emotional current that is fueling the behavior, most of us never successfully eliminate or change our negative defense mechanisms.

We must do some emotional archeology and dig beneath the surface if we are going to experience the real, lasting, change and EA we desire. We must look within ourselves to see what areas of our lives are not working. We must take back our power to claim the life we desire, and to determine what we need to do to change those areas.

Cultivating SAFE-T Within

I work with my clients to develop and build EA into their lives from the ground up. Health feels good, and health begets health. So, if we start by understanding the basic building blocks of EA in our lives as individuals—a process I call *SAFE-T*—we can begin incorporating them into our lives and create a safe place for us to thrive.

SAFE-T stands for:
S*TRIVING* to self-nurture
A*LIGNING* our emotional pipes
F*OSTERING* authenticity
E*NGAGING* in identity investment
T*REATING* past emotional wounds

Our individual journeys toward EA begin with **Striving** to nurture ourselves well. **Striving** to nurture is the *oxygen mask* that allows us to prioritize ourselves without feeling selfish or guilty. Certainly, only in caring for ourselves first can we care for and nurture others more authentically and effectively.

Once self-nurture is in place, we can begin to **Align** our emotional pipes, making sure our emotional plumbing is connected and in working order. Emotional alignment is vitally important so we can stay conjoined with our inner voice, name and manage our thoughts and feelings, and be able to speak them in a healthy, respectful way to the people around us.

If we attune ourselves to our thoughts and feelings, we can get to know ourselves in a new, much calmer way and to create a safe environment that can **Foster** authenticity. In identifying the negative, shaming, perfectionistic ways we experience ourselves that are the counterfeits of our authentic self, we can learn to speak the truth to ourselves in a much more kind, compassionate manner. Only by attuning ourselves can we get in touch with, embrace, and grow our true identity, which is rooted in our belovedness, our worth.

Subsequently, from a foundation of self-acceptance and authenticity, we can **Engage** in identity investment. We know how to invest. We invest in our 401(k), our house, our children's education. We even invest in the eventuality of our own deaths with life insurance. Yet there are very few people who commit the same time and energy into investing in their identities.

We are not static creatures. We are ever-changing, developing, and growing. Healthy individuals simply learn how to invest wisely in the process of identity development so their investment yields greater returns and dividends in their confidence, their competence, their ability to set and achieve goals, and their capacity to be in healthy relationships.

SAFE-T gradually moves us deeper into ourselves where we can safely begin to **Treat** past emotional wounds that remain. Sometimes we can identify and work through wounds alone as we walk on this journey. Sometimes having a guide to walk with us can be helpful–to encourage us, to safely nudge us, and to help us make the connections we need in order to unhook from the past events and painful wounds that have kept us stuck for so long.

The Benefits of Emotional Abundance

The idea that we can do something to create peace within ourselves is both hopeful and challenging–hopeful because we are no longer helpless spectators in the movie of our lives. We are active, powerful participants who *can* grow, who *can* become, and who *can* create a radically different way of living. This idea is also challenging because once we have the knowledge, and once we've begun to experience on the inside what health feels like, we can't go back.

If we begin to work out at the gym and feel the physical and emotional benefits of exercise, we're hooked. We want more. We like the way we feel, we love the energy we have, and we can't imagine going back to a sedentary lifestyle. EA works the same way. Once we begin building EA into our lives and start experiencing the benefits, we will want more. While physical exercise has known physical and emotional benefits, EA has benefits as well. Individuals who commit to EA increase their peace quotient. Their lives are calmer. They no longer experience the emotional roller coaster that once defined their lives and relationships. EA improves our emotional energy so we can create the life we want. We feel more confident in our competence to deal with the natural stresses of life.

EA impacts our children's EQ (emotional quotient); that is, the ability to recognize, evaluate, and manage their own emotions, as well as other's emotions. Parents are their children's primary teachers and role models for life and relationships. As we become healthier individuals and learn the skills to manage our emotions better and to engage in healthier relationships, our children will watch what we do and begin to mimic our words and actions. Thus, we are, in fact, modeling for our children how to be emotionally healthy individuals and have healthy relationships.

EA also inspires greater intimacy with our spouses. The safer we feel inside, the more open, authentic, and vulnerable we can be with our mates. The very act of owning responsibility for our emotional safety allows for much deeper, intimate connections in our marriages.

Lastly, EA allows us to integrate stability and peace in all of our relationships. When we have fostered peace internally, the stability and calm we feel as individuals has an overall ripple effect on all of our relationships. Our relationships have much less drama, and when issues arise, they are less intense and more manageable because we have developed an emotional tool belt with a variety of healthy coping skills to deal with and negotiate through conflict.

Now that we understand the goal, let's spend some time building our boat. Are you ready?

Chapter Seven

STRIVING TO SELF-NURTURE

Plant your own garden and decorate your own soul, instead of waiting for someone to bring you flowers.[28]

—Veronica Shoffstall

The Purpose of Self-Nurture

Self-nurture is the daily practice of learning how to be kind to myself—the prioritization of me emotionally. Before I leave for work in the morning, I may shower, do my make-up and hair, and iron my clothes in order to take care of myself physically. I may pack my lunch and heat a bowl of oatmeal in order to take care of myself nutritionally. As a spiritual being, I may also include a Bible reading or quiet time. But how many of us go through the day, week, month, even years without the slightest notion of caring for ourselves emotionally?

Emotionally abundant individuals have healthy habits built into their lives. One of those habits is that they have learned to

---

28 Veronica Shoffstall, *"Plant Your Own Garden,"* 1971.

incorporate self-nurture into their lives on a daily basis. Self-nurture isn't an all-day event. Self-nurture is simply fifteen to twenty minutes each day where we stop to process, or sort through, the events and emotions of the day. We defined Emotional Abundance (EA) earlier as the ability to feel our emotions, to reason through our emotions, to understand our emotions, and to effectively manage our emotions so we can appropriately respond to the people and circumstances around us. Self-nurture is the intentional time we create to make contact with, and process through, our emotions so we can manage them well.

Sounds easy enough, right? However, each time I introduce the practice of self-nurture to a client, the instinctive resistance in their response is amazing.

The reason is most of us are socialized to believe self-nurture is equal to being selfish. We actually feel better about ourselves when we perceive ourselves to be selfless or self-sacrificing. As parents, it seems there is a direct correlation between our worth and devotion as a parent and the time, energy, and resources we expend in service to our children. The more we sacrifice, the better we feel about ourselves as parents.

In addition, self-nurture conjures up images of laziness. In a culture where the word *busy* has become synonymous with importance and value, many find difficulty in caring for themselves without feeling either selfish or lazy or perhaps both. Thus the demands of daily life seem to trap us on the conveyer belt of human *doing*, so much so we are never allowed to experience ourselves as human *beings*.

Living on Empty

In reality, we were not created to be the Energizer Bunny or robots. We each have an emotional fuel tank, and for too many of us, the tank is below empty. We are running on fumes. As a result, prescriptions for anti-anxiety and anti-depression medication are at an all-time high.

While for some medication is absolutely necessary and beneficial, there are many of us who use medication as an energy drink to keep us pumped up so we can grind out life for one more day. Too many of us wonder why, when we have everything we ever dreamed of, are we so depressed? Even though we love our spouses and our children, our careers and our friends, why do we still feel so empty inside? Why does everything feel so overwhelming?

The truth is I cannot be the best mother, wife, lover, worker, or friend until I have first become the best *me*. I cannot give anything to anyone around me unless and until I have first given to myself.

The Oxygen Mask

Have you ever been on a flight and watched the flight attendant giving the pre-flight safety instructions? At a certain point in their presentation, they pull out the oxygen mask and demonstrate how to put the mask over your face should the cabin lose air pressure. The flight attendant instructs passengers to put the oxygen mask over their own faces before assisting their child with an oxygen mask.

You might think to yourself, *No, as a good mother, I would make sure my child had his or her safety mask on before putting one on myself.* That would appear to be the most loving, selfless act, right?

Unfortunately, in a crisis situation where every second is vital, there is a likelihood that I cannot get their oxygen mask on appropriately, therefore putting both our lives in jeopardy. However, if I can manipulate my mask quickly enough, I will have time to adjust my child's mask and ensure a greater chance for survival. In essence, *the* most loving thing I can do to care for and protect my child is to care for and protect myself so I am in a position to care for them as well.

This may sound like heresy, especially to those of us who were raised in the church, but caring for ourselves first is indeed valid. When we look at Jesus' life, there were countless times He withdrew from teaching, healing, and ministering to people in order to spend time with his Father – to refuel – so He could accomplish His Father's ultimate mission for His life here on earth.

The same applies to us in our lives and missions. No matter what we are passionate about, no matter whom we serve or how we give, that we learn how to give to ourselves first is imperative and the only way to truly make a difference in our families or communities. Caring for ourselves first is also the only way we are going to survive. Thus, as emotionally-abundant individuals, we must learn how to embrace *self-nurture* as a gift to those we love and begin to incorporate nurturing ourselves into our lives.

The Practice of Self-Nurture

Many activities can be self-nurturing such as working out, taking a walk, journaling, sipping a hot cup of tea, or taking a hot bath at the end of the day. What makes an activity self-nurture as opposed to exercise or activity is *how* we do it.

Good exercise may involve going to the gym or taking a long walk with loud music blaring in my ears, but it will not make for good self-nurture. Taking a hot bath or trying to journal with kids running in and out, or with the TV blaring may be beneficial on some level, but will not be good self-nurture.

Self-nurture requires me to create a quiet space for myself so I can process my emotions. Through self-nurturing activities, I can arrive at thought-filled, meaningful decisions based on reflective emotional awareness, rather than trying to repress my deep thoughts and emotions or carry them around with me. I am able to listen to and validate my emotions. Then by engaging my mind to think through my emotions, I am able to get some distance from my emotions and make decisions for my life that value and respect both my thoughts and feelings. This allows me to build balance and creative solution-building into my daily life. While solitude connects me with my Creator, self-nurture connects me with myself. Both are necessary if we desire to build EA into our lives and relationships.

Let me be clear: self-nurture is not a synonym for self-centeredness. Self-nurture is not an excuse to indulge myself in whatever impulse I might have. Self-nurture is not a blanket permission slip to ignore my responsibilities to my work, my family, or my friends. Self-nurture is simply a time I take each and every day to continue my personal discovery process.

Furthermore, I cannot share an opinion in the boardroom, living room, or bedroom if I haven't spent time alone connecting with and understanding my own thoughts and feelings. I cannot allow myself to be intimately known by another person if I haven't first spent time becoming intimately acquainted with myself. Indeed, drawing healthy boundaries for myself in a relationship would be impossible if I didn't know what I felt like when a boundary had been crossed.

Self-nurture thus becomes the emotional radar and rudder of our internal ships. Self-nurture develops the habit of knowing when something unpleasant or unsettling has happened and allows us to make minor, daily adjustments so we can achieve our goals and avoid as much unnecessary drama and conflict along the way. More importantly, as we are continually in the process of discovering new things about ourselves, self-nurture allows us to dream new dreams, to plot new courses, and to build the courage to live this adventure to the fullest, one day at a time, one step at a time.

Stepping Stones

- Identify three or four self-nurture activities that you could begin to incorporate into your schedule. Notice what activities seem to be the best fit for you and your lifestyle.

- Begin your self-nurture time by reflecting back over the events of the day. Next, identify how you felt about those events as well as what you thought about the events.

- Lastly, how did you feel about *you* in those events? Did you feel anxious, uncertain, proud, or strong? Is there anything you would like to have handled differently? How might you do things differently in the future?

Chapter Eight

Aligning Our Emotional Pipes

Unexpressed emotions will never die. They are buried alive and will come forth later in uglier ways.[29]

—Sigmund Freud

Growing Up as a Plumber's Kid

When I was growing up, my dad was a plumber. Talk of flappers, traps, valves, drain fields, seals, connections, and fittings was normal conversation at the dinner table. My dad loved his job and was devoted to excellence in everything he did.

Dad would often take my brother and me with him to work, partially to instill in us a strong work ethic, and partially to educate us with the hope that one day, one of us might want to follow in his footsteps. Okay. Maybe the hope was more about my brother following in his footsteps and I was just a tag-along, but let's not tarnish a memory!

---

29 Sigmund Freud. QuotesWave.com. Accessed June 5, 2014.

I wanted so much to please my dad and learn whatever he was teaching, but as soon as he would explain something, I would forget what he told me almost as quickly. He could show me an Allen wrench or a tube cutter and, ten minutes later, I'd have a distinct look of confusion on my face when he asked me to hand him one.

What I remember most from those days with my dad is he always gave me the job of painting the ends of the PVC pipes with purple primer. I somehow felt that my job must be incredibly important, so I worked diligently to be the best purple-primer painter anywhere.

Obviously, I was not exactly mechanically inclined, but what I did learn from those experiences with my dad was that the way the pipes worked had a profound impact on the overall functioning of a house. If the pipes were laid out, connected, and sealed properly, the plumbing would function well. However, if there was a leak or a stoppage, the flaw would affect everything else around that failure in the system. You might not see the cause, but a leak could destroy the structure all around and result in an expensive repair.

Our Emotional Plumbing System

Our emotional interior is much like the interior of a house. We, too, have emotional pipes that if connected, flowing, and functioning properly, allow our individual selves to function at optimal performance. However, if there is a leak or blockage in our emotional pipes, the result is either a flood or a back-up. For some, there is a complete emotional disconnect. Sadly, they feel that if they can cut themselves off entirely from their emotions, they will never have to experience the potential pain or messiness that can result as a consequence of feeling.

Yet even for those who have cut themselves off entirely from their emotions, the emotions don't simply disappear. They will drain into, contaminate, and infect some area of their lives whether they want them to or not.

That is why, in our desire to find peace with ourselves and develop Emotional Abundance (EA) – being able to feel our emotions, to reason through our emotions, to understand our emotions, and to effectively manage our emotions so we can appropriately respond to the people and circumstances around us – doing an emotional plumbing inspection is so important. We need to see if everything is in working order and if there are any stoppages or leaks, so we can get our emotional pipes connected and functioning well.

If you have begun the process of self-nurture, you are well on the road to creating an ideal environment to connect your emotional pipes in a healthy way. That is because in order to plug into our feelings, we must have a quiet, safe environment where we can connect with and experience our emotions. Self-nurture provides exactly such an environment.

Many individuals can experience difficulties assessing their levels of emotional connection. If you struggle to describe what you're feeling and always rely on what you're thinking, you are probably disconnected from your emotions. If the only emotion you can articulate is frustration, you could be disconnected from your emotions. Once, when I was describing to a client the most common places we feel emotions in our bodies, I placed my hand on my stomach. Looking at me quizzically, he stated, "I've never felt anything there except indigestion."

Building Our Emotional Vocabulary

Learning to connect with our emotions can be a new and quite challenging experience. Yet the more we can become aware of the specific emotions we are feeling and process them, the more we will be able to work through them productively and to calm ourselves through the emotion.

Processing is the ability to connect with our emotions directly and efficiently, think through them, and purge them, so we are no longer forced to carry the emotional residue around with us. Remember, if we do nothing with them, our emotions don't just disappear, they simply pile up one on top of another, until they eventually explode or implode. Processing is one skill that gets our emotions up and out, which allows us to create a place of balance between our thinking and feeling.

I've included a list of emotions, as described by W. Gerrod Parrot in his book *The Emotions in Social Psychology* (2001)[30], to help us begin to categorize our primary emotions and to see how they can be subdivided into more specific secondary emotions, which themselves can be subdivided into more specific tertiary emotions. Only by understanding the depth of our emotions as well as the connection between the different layers of our emotions, can we free ourselves from the hold they can have on us at times.

---

30 W. Gerrod Parrot, *The Emotions in Social Psychology: Essential Readings* (Philadelphia, PA: Psychology Press, 2001).

PRIMARY EMOTION	SECONDARY EMOTION	TERTIARY EMOTIONS
LOVE	AFFECTION	Adoration, affection, love, fondness, liking, attraction, caring, tenderness, compassion, sentimentality
	LUST	Arousal, desire, lust, passion, infatuation
	LONGING	Longing
JOY	CHEERFULNESS	Amusement, bliss, cheerfulness, gaiety, glee, jolliness, joviality, joy, delight, enjoyment, gladness, happiness, jubilation, elation, satisfaction, ecstasy, euphoria
	ZEST	Enthusiasm, zeal, zest, excitement, thrill, exhilaration
	CONTENTMENT	Contentment, pleasure
	PRIDE	Pride, triumph
	OPTIMISM	Eagerness, hope, optimism
	ENTHRALLMENT	Enthrallment, rapture
	RELIEF	Relief
SURPRISE	SURPRISE	Amazement, surprise, astonishment
ANGER	IRRITATION	Aggravation, irritation, agitation, annoyance, grouchiness, grumpiness
	EXASPERATION	Exasperation, frustration
	RAGE	Anger, rage, outrage, fury, wrath, hostility, ferocity, bitterness, hate, loathing, scorn, spite, vengefulness, dislike, resentment
	DISGUST	Disgust, revulsion, contempt
	ENVY	Envy, jealousy
	TORMENT	Torment

SADNESS	SUFFERING	Agony, suffering, hurt, anguish
	SADNESS	Depression, despair, hopelessness, gloom, glumness, sadness, unhappiness, grief, sorrow, woe, misery, melancholy
	DISAPPOINTMENT	Dismay, disappointment, displeasure
	SHAME	Guilt, shame, regret, remorse
	NEGLECT	Alienation, isolation, neglect, loneliness, rejection, homesickness, defeat, dejection, insecurity, embarrassment, humiliation, insult
	SYMPATHY	Pity, sympathy
FEAR	HORROR	Alarm, shock, fear, fright, horror, terror, panic, hysteria, mortification
	NERVOUSNESS	Anxiety, nervousness, tenseness, uneasiness, apprehension, worry, distress, dread

As you go through your day and in your self-nurture time, begin to identify exactly what you are feeling from all three levels of emotion (tertiary emotions, secondary emotions, and primary emotions). Try to be as specific as possible. The broader your emotional vocabulary, the better-equipped you will be in communicating your emotions accurately to others and the more effective you will be in identifying what action, if any, is needed to resolve that emotion.

Making contact with your emotions, learning how to quiet yourself enough to listen, experience, and process your emotions, not only nurtures EA, but opens the door to a sacred place where your inner voice lives.

Learning to Listen to Our Inner Voice

Deep inside each of us is a voice – a quiet, respectful, non-in-trusive voice – that acts somewhat like an internal GPS system. If we lean in and quiet all of the chatter that incessantly distracts us, we can hear this voice. Some people call it our *instinct*. As a Christian, I call the voice the Holy Spirit. As Jesus promised, He resides in us, just to bring comfort, help, direction, wisdom, and guidance for our life's journey. (John 14:26 NIV)

This inner voice can only be heard once we've connected our emotional pipes. Although the voice is not the voice of our emotions, its residence is deep within us. If we've shut ourselves off from our emotions, chances are high we've shut ourselves off from that voice as well.

As a result of painful, traumatic experiences, many people have learned to completely shut down their emotions as a survival skill. Others learn to live life disconnected from their emotions because they have been taught by their families of origin that emotions are bad (either verbally or nonverbally). They think they hear their inner voice. They believe this is the voice of logic and reason. They like to listen to this voice because listening keeps them at a comfortable distance from everything that isn't clear-cut, black or white. Yet the voice of logic and reason, more sophisticated perhaps than our emotional voice, is not our inner voice anymore than the voice of emotion is.

Just as some people have been completely cut off from their emotions, others have been entirely lost in their emotions and overwhelmed by them. For a variety of reasons, they have never learned how to adequately calm or regulate their emotions. As a result, the volume of feeling is so high, the quality of thinking so distracted and disorganized, they cannot hear the voice inside either.

As we develop EA, our job is to find that place right in the middle of our thinking and feeling, which allows us to feel our emotions and calm them. Once we have done that, we can use our thinking to process through our emotions and arrive at a centered, peaceful place. Only then will we be quiet enough in our hearts and our minds to hear our inner voice, to listen to the whispered words of encouragement and direction offered for the steps that lie ahead.

Regardless of how or when our inner voice operates, the fact is only when we embrace solitude and self-nurture as daily practices, will we create the space to hear this voice. My inner voice hadn't remained silent from me. The truth is I wasn't listening. I had never tuned in to hear. Yet, what once was just a faint whisper, grew stronger and more clear to me over time.

For a long time, even when my inner voice spoke to me, I would second-guess what I heard. I would rationalize all of the reasons why the voice couldn't be right, why I must not listen.

Sometimes I would just ignore this voice altogether. I would make decisions based on my emotions. I would follow my heart, my feelings, the places where all of my compulsive impulses dwell, and I would make decisions without using my thinking to process through my emotions. That pattern led to many destructive outcomes.

There were other times I would listen to a friend, a pastor, a family member's voice and trust their voice as if it were my own. Unfortunately, though wisdom from others can be valuable, I can never use others as a crutch that prevents me from finding my own inner voice, and learning to listen. Now I am learning how to be in healthy contact with this voice. I trust this voice more and more each day.

Certainly, this entire discussion of emotions, thoughts, and our inner voice is not an end in and of itself. Getting our emotional pipes connected and in working order is simply a step toward creating EA and maintaining a healthy, functional emotional plumbing system.

Owning Responsibility For Our Emotions

Learning to connect with and distinguish my thoughts and feelings is necessary so I can do something with them. My emotions are not the responsibility of anyone on the planet other than me. Whether I'm feeling happy or sad, anxious or angry, I own my emotions, and I alone am responsible for my emotions. That means I am responsible for my happiness. My husband is not. My boss is not. My best friend is not. No one is emotionally responsible for me but me.

If I am not happy, my responsibility is to identify what is contributing to my unhappiness and be able to determine what changes I may need to make to decrease my sadness and increase my joy. Giving someone else the responsibility for my emotional well-being is the definition of codependency. Health allows me to hold that power for myself.

Learning How to Manage Our Emotions

When I began to own responsibility for my emotions, I felt much less helpless inside, much less out-of-control. I felt I could actually calm myself. I could breathe deeply, I could take a time-out for solitude or self-nurture. I could feel my body relax, and my mind settle. I began to experience peace – in little glimpses, like tiny beams of light sparkling in hopeless places.

This peace, this abundance only comes as we learn to calm ourselves and manage our emotions. We cannot process or think through our emotions as long as their intensity is high. Our brain shuts down. Our minds become flooded. Once we can calm ourselves, we can effectively process our emotions and find the best solution to resolve that emotion.

As I process my emotions, I ask myself a series of questions. What am I feeling? Why am I feeling this? What is this emotion about? Where did this come from? What do I need to do with this emotion to resolve it? Do I need healing from a past painful experience? Is this a situation over which I have no control? Is there an aspect over which I do have control? Is there something I can learn from this experience? Is there something I could have done differently or could do differently in the future? Is there someone with whom I need to speak? If so, what is the message I need to share? Lastly, for whom or for what can I pray?

You don't have to be afraid of your emotions. You don't have to live life disconnected from them. Emotions are God-given. They are powerful. Connect your emotional pipes well. Turn on the water. Let them flow.

You can experience abundance in your emotions. Pull out some purple-primer paint, we've got some plumbing to do!

Stepping Stones

- How well are you connected to your emotions?

- Are you able to name your feelings specifically?

- In what ways have you made others responsible for your emotional well-being?

- How easy or difficult do you find experiencing your emotions and calming yourself in them?

- Where is your favorite place to process your feelings?

- What prevents you from coming into contact with your inner voice?

- Do you have a tendency to trust your inner voice, second-guess yourself, or depend on someone else's voice to make decisions?

Chapter Nine

Fostering Authenticity

The thing that is really hard, and really amazing, is giving up on being perfect and beginning the work of becoming yourself.[31]

—Anna Quindlen

Living in a Counterfeit World

Let's face it. All of us at some point, whether we knew or not, have bought a counterfeit. Whether we were looking for a lower-cost prescription medication or simply trying to obtain some designer watch, handbag, or boots at a discount price, we have all been duped by an imposter that looked just like the real thing. If we're honest, many of us don't mind being duped. We have lost an appreciation for what's real because we just want what we want—easy, fast, and cheap. Who cares if the item is real, right—as long as the look of status we're hoping for is supported?

---

31 Anna Quindlen, *Commencement speech* (May 23, 1999). http://www.keelynet.com/quin.htm.

Unfortunately, counterfeiting hasn't just impacted the world of luxury goods. Over the past few decades, the practice has filtered down into our medications, our food supply, even our home-building materials. What is the saddest to me, though, is the way counterfeiting has begun to impact our relationships and even our individual identities.

With the increasing popularity of social networks, we can now even counterfeit friends and relationships. People are engaged to, and in love with, others on Facebook who they have never met and who don't even exist. Even the idea of posting status updates makes us feel pressured to present ourselves and our lives as an ideal picture of who we are, or who we would like others to think we are. We become satisfied with a world of pretend people with pretend identities living in pretend relationships.

Nothing Will Satisfy Like the Real Thing

The problem with spending so much time and energy creating or living an illusion is we never get to experience the real thing. Somewhere in all of us is a longing for something authentic, something dependable. Nothing fake will ever satisfy our souls like a true connection with a friend, a genuine encounter with God, or an authentic understanding of ourselves.

So why would anyone settle for a counterfeit when they could have the real thing? We all desire a safe place to be accepted, valued, and loved for who we are. But we are afraid that who we are is simply not enough. Therefore, in order to avoid risking potential rejection or ridicule, we unconsciously build walls that keep everyone at a safe distance. We allow them to see only what we want them to see.

Somewhere in the transaction, we fail to get to know our true, authentic selves. We unconsciously choose the safety of a counterfeit self with all of our defenses in place to protect us, and our shiny façade in place to perfect us. If we don't begin to explore who we are, and learn how to accept and love ourselves, we will never experience an authentic sense of self that comes from within. We will never find Emotional Abundance (EA). We will never find peace.

The Risk of the Inner Journey

A huge risk is involved then, to move beyond simply looking externally to find our identity and happiness, to looking within ourselves to discover the essence of those very things. Our true identity never lies on the outside; we can only find our *real* self within.

Our greatest fear as Brennan Manning ponders, "is that as I expose the imposter and lay bare my true self, I will be abandoned by my friends and ridiculed by my enemies."[32] Somehow in our efforts to be what everyone else thought we should be, we miss out on discovering ourselves, whom God created us to be.

Caught in the cycle of looking to others to provide our sense of self-worth and happiness, we never allow ourselves the experience of moving deeper inside, closer to the person we truly are before God. This can be scary, for as Margaret Silf shares:

As I begin to see who I am — truly and without protective masks — I may find serious discrepancies between the person who lives in the Where [in their circumstances] and the person God created me to be, in my deepest self. I will find shame, but I will also find glory. I will

32 Brennan Manning, *Abba's Child* (Colorado Springs, CO: NavPress, 1994), 89.

move closer to the God who dwells in my heart and the encounter will challenge me in ways that I cannot predict ... [This] is the risk of the inner journey.[33]

If we can focus our energies, during whatever our season of life, on building our foundation and securing our identity, then everything else we build on top—our relationships, our careers, our finances, and so forth—will be built well, resting on a solid foundation. If we do not, we will eventually experience collapse.

I have experienced collapse. I have experienced building all of my identity, security, and peace on a foundation of the applause and approval of others. Those things are intoxicating drugs when they exist, but they are equally as deadly and destructive when they do not.

How To Spot a Counterfeit

Our first task then is to be able to identify our counterfeit or *false self.* The actual definition of the word *counterfeit* according to Merriam Webster's Dictionary, is something, "made in imitation of something else, with the intent to deceive."[34]

So who is your counterfeit? What do they look like? How do they behave? There are several clues that could indicate you may be living out of your counterfeit self.

Counterfeits Are Never Real

In my own life, my counterfeit began to grow long ago in my childhood as a way of dealing with the world around me. I learned

---

33 Margaret Silf, *Inner Compass* (Chicago, IL: Loyola Press, 1999).
34 "Counterfeit." *Merriam-Webster.com.* Merriam-Webster, n.d. Web. 2 Dec. 2014.
<http://www.merriam-webster.com/dictionary/counterfeit>.

early on as I experienced taunting and ridicule from my peers in school that being me was not safe. In order to gain their approval and be accepted in their circle, I needed to be different than I was.

I needed to look differently, dress differently, and even talk differently if I was to *fit in*. I don't even know exactly how I changed; all I know is I slowly left the place where I owned myself and began becoming what others expected of me so I might feel accepted.

Lisa's Story

I learned as a young child that I needed to be special; I needed to perform well in order to get the love and approval for which I was so desperate. If others didn't think I was good enough, I had to do better, be better, be *perfect* and then they would see that I was worthy of their love.

A story from my childhood was pivotal in birthing my counterfeit and creating a perfect environment for her to flourish. Chris—my brother whom I love, respect, and adore—is two years older than me and was discovered early on to be a prodigy on the piano. As a result, he always found favor wherever he went. He played professionally as a child and was admired for his many gifts. Chris was special and loved by everyone who met him.

I took piano lessons right alongside my brother, but what took him ten minutes to learn and perfect took me ten hours to learn and perfect. I persevered. I won my share of awards in the various competitions in which we participated, but piano-playing never came easily for me.

On my first day of junior high school, I was so excited for 6th period to arrive, as this was to be my first day in the McLane

Junior High School Choir. As we all crowded into the room and took our seats, the choir director, Ms. Clawsen, began to call the roll. When she got to my name she stammered, "Lisa Springer (my maiden name)! Lisa Springer! Are you Chris Springer's sister?" Before I could even reply, with the choir standing in their respective sections, she had ushered me to the piano, and was giving me the downbeat to the 1970s radio hit, *And I'd Really Love to See You Tonight.*

Everything was good for the first four bars. I was even feeling I might be able to pull this thing off when the ground began to give way around me and I crashed and burned in the figurative, humiliating, death-defying sense. What I remember most was Ms. Clawsen lowering her baton, looking at me, and flatly stating, "Oh, I guess you're not your brother."

The sting of that moment changed the way I experienced everything from then on, especially the way I experienced myself. At that moment, I began living out of a need to receive others' approval, respect, and love. At that moment, I left myself and began to embrace my counterfeit self because that was easier, perhaps safer than experiencing the pain of my authentic self being rejected.

Counterfeits Live in Fear

Because of the experience of being rejected, I became determined to avoid that same pain again. I was desperate to achieve the acceptance of others thinking that their approval of me would take away the pain. And sometimes, as long as I *performed perfectly,* I would gain their approval and feel a cessation of the pain.

But what happens when we can't perform perfectly? If we can't maintain their approval, the consequences can be devastating. We will have to experience their rejection of us all over again. That pain is too much to deal with, so we stay trapped on this hamster wheel of deception. All the while we think we're deceiving others. Who we're really deceiving is ourselves.

My counterfeit is perpetually petrified this illusion I've created will be exposed, like my piano skills, and everyone will discover the fraud I truly am and reject me altogether. As Brennan Manning beautifully details, "Living out of the false self creates a compulsive desire to present a perfect image to the public so that everyone will admire us and no one will know us. The imposter's life becomes a perpetual roller-coaster ride of elation and depression."[35]

Sadly, this was my experience and is the experience of many today.

Because we live in fear, we find saying no to bosses, spouses, children, even well-meaning church committees difficult. In an effort to please everyone around us, we end up exhausted, empty, and resentful.

Counterfeits Lie

From the time I was small, there was a tape-recorder in my mind that began to record and play back messages to me about myself. Usually, the messages were neither kind nor accepting. These messages sounded something like this: *You'll never be good enough. You're worthless. You're stupid. No one will ever love you. You can't do anything right. If you were only smarter, cuter, taller, thinner, etc., others would like you. You'll never amount to anything.* These

---

35 Brennan Manning, *Abba's Child* (Colorado Springs, CO: NavPress, 1994), 31.

messages were lies that bombarded my mind from the time I woke up to the time I went to sleep. If we're honest, we could fill an entire book with the lies that play in our heads all day every day.

These thoughts are relentless, they are unyielding, and yes, they are lies. But I am continually amazed how powerful these lies are, shaping and molding our image, our value as individuals, and our worth as human beings. We believe them. We hear them so much they become the truth out of which we live.

These lies are not God the Creator's truth about us, but because we have listened to them and wandered away from our inner selves, the lies seem easier to believe than the truth. They also have a way of becoming self-fulfilling prophesies. The more I listen to the counterfeit's lies, the more I believe them; the more I make decisions based on them, the more I experience the negative outcome that follows. My pastor laid out a fitting equation that states, negative thought → negative decision → negative habit → negative character → negative destiny.

With those lies, I remain defeated. My counterfeit keeps me from getting to know who I am, the person whom God sees—my truest and deepest self, one who is loved and delighted in by her Father.

Counterfeits Are Well-Defended

Have you ever met someone who simply cannot take criticism, who becomes defensive, defeated, broken, or angry at any correction or advice no matter how lovingly or carefully delivered? These are not narcissists who genuinely believe they are special, thus more knowledgeable and skillful than others. These are people like I used to be; individuals who have such a fragile sense of self that any negative input feels so threatening and painful, their counterfeits create walls and defenses to protect against the perceived potential threat or injury. As children, we may have needed these coping skills to keep us safe. As adults, those same coping skills aren't working for us or our relationships.

Counterfeits Cannot Be Alone

My counterfeit needs attention. She craves attention. She demands to be noticed. Her craving for validation becomes an addiction that can never be satisfied.

Being alone brings my counterfeit face to face with my own nothingness, the vacuum where my true self should reside but instead is only an empty shadow exposing my intolerable shame. Nothingness is to be avoided at all costs. I will run to relationships to escape aloneness. I will run to food. I will run to just about anything including spending, alcohol, work, or exercise in order to avoid having to face the truth of my bandaged, broken self.

My counterfeit does not want me to learn how to create a more compassionate environment for my authentic self to heal and grow strong. Perhaps then I would no longer need her.

So, if my counterfeit is not the real me, who is the real me? There are five truths that form the foundation of my identity. The more I understand these truths and apply them, the more my counterfeit will start to fade into the background, and my authentic self will emerge beautiful and strong, just as God created.

My Authentic Self Knows Its Worth

The real me is the me that existed before everything else began to introduce words of unworthiness and unkindness into my emotional consciousness and vocabulary. The real me was the little tow-headed, freckle-faced girl who was cuddled in her aunt's lap, completely unaware of anything other than being loved and being safe. Nothing else existed in those moments.

The real me today, as a result of my own journey, is a woman who knows her belovedness. When I began to take the energy I was expending to get approval or affirmation from everyone around me, and instead channeled that energy internally, speaking to myself the words of affirmation and acceptance for which I was so hungry, I became less hungry.

As I grew satisfied and full inside, my center of gravity began to shift from being a tetherball, forever knocked around by the winds and wounds of other people, to being the tetherball pole, where I was centered. I was no longer at the mercy of something or someone else exerting their will on me. My power was cemented in God. I was grounded.

Interestingly, because I needed outside approval less, I no longer felt the pain of their rejection or the need for perfection. Therefore, I could give myself permission *not* to be perfect. I could experience myself as completely imperfect and beloved at the same time. My belovedness was no longer the end goal I was driven to attain in order to earn or claim my worth or identity. My belovedness simply was my identity–period.

My belovedness was the place out of which everything else in life flowed. Life became much calmer, infinitely more peaceful, and satisfying. I was experiencing EA. I had nothing left to prove.

I felt as if someone told me I could finally get off the rollercoaster I'd been living on for most of my life. I could finally breathe.

Today, I wouldn't want to go back to that life for anything. Today I can choose to ride a rollercoaster, and I can choose to get off one. But my life is no longer a rollercoaster, and that's worth the price of admission!

My Authentic Self Is Unafraid

My authentic self no longer lives in fear. When I stopped living out of a need for outside approval and was no longer driven to be perfect, I began to feel safe with myself for the first time.

There is a direct relationship between how safe I feel with myself and how safe I feel with God. If I am rejecting and unkind with myself, I will most likely perceive God to be rejecting and unkind toward me. Conversely, if I am kind and accepting of myself, I will most likely experience God as being kind toward me and accepting of me as well.

This applies to my relationships with others, too. If I'm critical of myself, I will naturally perceive others to be more critical of me. The fact is I can only feel safe with others to the extent that I feel safe with myself. Otherwise, I will give my friends too much power to shape me, define me, and consequently, make me feel safe. I think I unconsciously believed if they made me feel safe, then perhaps I would be okay.

Today I find I don't fear people nearly as much. Their reactions or responses to me don't hold as much weight because they no longer have the job of making me feel safe. I make myself feel safe. And the safer I feel, the more I can allow my authentic self to emerge and to flourish in the rich soil of self-acceptance, nourished by God's unconditional love.

I give myself permission to be imperfect and yet trust I am still worthy, still loved. The reason I can do this is my identity is no longer based on my performance; my identity is based on my position to the Father. Just as I will always be the daughter of Chuck and Pat Springer, so I will always be the *beloved* of my Heavenly Father.

My Authentic Self Speaks the Truth

My authentic self is truthful. Not everything that runs through my mind is the truth, but my authentic self is better able to *take captive every thought to make it obedient to Christ* (2 Corinthians 10:5 NIV). The more I am able to identify the lies playing in my head, which have kept me defeated for so long, the more I can identify them, and the more I can begin to speak the truth to them.

This is where some people get off track. When I say that I speak the truth to the lies, that doesn't mean the *power-of-positive thinking* or *Pollyanna* kind of truth. The truth is, I can tell myself all day long I look just like Gisele Bundchen, or I'm the smartest there ever was, but that kind of desired truth comes crashing down when I wake up and look in the mirror or get my test scores back on my college entrance exams.

That's not the truth I'm talking about. What I'm describing here is the kind of truth that's a balanced and accurate truth – the only truth I can buy into that doesn't force me to avoid every mirror, every test, or every illusion I've created. When I can identify the lie that plays through my mind, I can begin to speak the truth to the lie and create a *self-talk* that is much more kind, more compassionate, and generally more positive.

The truth is I'm no supermodel and I'll never be the smartest kid in town, but the truth also is, that's okay. The truth is I like the way I look. There are some things I can't change, but there are some I can enhance or minimize. The truth is I don't need to look like Gisele Bundchen in order to have friends. If I do, they're probably not true friends. The truth is, though I don't have the IQ of Einstein, I always do my best, and I like that about me. The truth is, if I do my best, that's all God asks, and the rest is out of my control.

The more we develop the discipline of filtering our thoughts and creating a balanced, truthful dialog with ourselves, the less we remain captive to the irrational, critical condemnation of the lies. We create the script by which we think, relate, and live. Is your script based on the truth, or is the script based on the lies with which the enemy has attempted to destroy you?

My Authentic Self Needs No Defenses

My authentic self no longer needs protective armor or defensiveness. Because I have done the work of building a strong inner self, I am able to feel safer with myself and others. Therefore, I no longer need the walls or defenses that at one time were crucial to my very survival.

There are times when individuals are unhappy with me, are critical of me, or feel hurt by me. These experiences are realities for anyone who is in a relationship with another human being. Having a strong inner core allows me to listen to negative feedback. I can reflect and evaluate whether what is being shared is accurate or not, whether I have ownership/responsibility for the problem or not, and from there find the greatest place of EA for me in the situation.

If the negative feedback is accurate, I am strong enough and safe enough to own responsibility for my actions or words. I can apologize (if that's appropriate to the situation) and formulate a plan to correct or improve the issue. The important thing is I can be open to my mistakes or weaknesses, because they no longer define my worth. I understand I'm on a lifelong journey and I will always be growing and learning. Therefore a mistake, instead of requiring condemnation, is an opportunity for growth.

Likewise, when listening to negative feedback, I may find the negative feedback is not accurate and I don't have ownership of the problem. Such times can be even more challenging. The temptation is to either become angry and defensive at the other person or to abandon myself entirely to them, accepting their truth as my truth and owning responsibility for something over which I have no responsibility. Doing so just to *keep the peace* doesn't ever keep the peace.

When we own responsibility for something that is not ours to own, the conflict that exists inside of us will grow into resentment and bitterness. Eventually the conflict will either explode externally onto that person or onto someone else who just happens to be in the wrong place at the wrong time, or implode internally, taking a sledgehammer or wrecking ball to one more interior wall of our foundation or sense of self. Neither feels good. Both are destructive patterns that lead to greater amounts of unhealth and unpeace in our lives.

There is a way you can listen to another person's criticisms or complaints. You can sit with them, you can listen to them, and after taking the time to reflect, if you find no ownership for the problem, you can lovingly and respectfully affirm their friendship. You can validate their feelings, and at the same time calmly state your inability to own what is not yours to own. You can walk away from the situation respecting the other person as well as yourself.

My Authentic Self Loves Solitude

Lastly, my authentic self can be alone. As I have strengthened the foundation of my identity and sense of self, I have come to experience my aloneness not as the wound of loneliness, but as the gift of solitude. I no longer have to erect external supports—people, accomplishments, money or position—to escape the void that exists deep within.

As I have come face to face with my own nothingness, my mere humanity, my distinct lack of perfection, and the anxiety that arises in coming face to face with this unfamiliar stranger, I have been freed.

To stop running and finally accept reality is freeing. To recognize and identify the damage that exists in my interior self is freeing. Simply to breathe, and know that I don't have to keep up the charade any longer, is freeing. I have a Heavenly Father, who will walk with me and work with me while I slowly, deliberately find and rebuild the foundation of my true self.

Somewhere in the process, as I pick up the shards of brokenness that lie everywhere around me, I find that I have the courage not only to accept this new reality, but to embrace the pieces of rubble as a beautiful mosaic.

Today I love my alone time. I find peace in solitude. I discover new places inside of me that God is waiting to explore with me, to birth new passions and new purposes. I am broken yet whole, plain yet beautiful, imperfect yet beloved. What peace to realize that I do not fear my counterfeit anymore, and more importantly, that I do not need my counterfeit anymore.

As you begin to see where the counterfeit parts of yourself are, you can create an environment that is much kinder and more compassionate where you can discover and foster authenticity. In a world of counterfeits, there truly is nothing like the real thing.

....

Stepping Stones

- When did you start being what others wanted of you instead of being yourself?

- Where do you look to get validation or approval?

- How has fear prevented you from feeling safe with others, yourself and God?

- How has perfectionism driven you in your life and relationships?

- What are the lies that have kept you buying counterfeit?

- In your journal, begin to write down the negative thoughts about yourself that play through your head on a daily basis. In a separate column, practice writing down truth statements next to each negative thought or lie. Remember that a truth statement isn't simply the equal opposite, nor is such a statement the *power of positive thinking* approach. Truth statements should be balanced statements that do not fall into one extreme or another. They are truths that you can believe.

- What are the truths about your authentic self? Begin speaking the truths to yourself instead of waiting for others to speak them to you.

- How do you respond to criticism? What are your defense mechanisms of choice – denial, rationalization, projection, blaming, defensiveness, contempt, anger, shutting down or introjection – where you adopt someone else's values or perspective without ever exploring whether or not they fit you?

- Do you find being alone difficult? Do you experience your alone time as loneliness or solitude?

Chapter Ten

Engaging Identity Investment

Every one of us has in him a continent of undiscovered character.
Blessed is he who acts the Columbus to his own soul.[36]

—Charles L. Wallis

The Value of Investing

When we become passionate about something, we are willing to invest in our passion. I'm passionate about my children, so I'm willing to invest myself in their lives and education. I'm passionate about my faith, so I'm willing to invest myself in my faith. I'm passionate about my friendships, so I invest myself in them. I'm not passionate about exercise though I know I should be. Therefore, I haven't invested in a great pair of running shoes. Hopefully I will be able to retire one day, so I have become reluctantly passionate about my 401(k).

No matter what we're doing, we invest in order to yield a certain return on our investment. We invest in our children with the hope

---

36 Charles L. Wallis, *Words of Life* (Harper & Row, 1966).

our energy and resources will yield successful, happy futures for them. We invest in our faith in order to grow into mature, strong people of faith who can impact our families and communities for Christ. We invest in our friendships so we will have deep, meaningful contact and support throughout the difficult seasons of our lives. We invest in exercise in order to be physically fit and healthy. We invest in our retirements so one day hopefully we won't have to work, and we can enjoy the fruits of our labor.

Prioritizing Identity Investment

Identity investing works the same way and is as important as every other type of investing we do. The problem is we simply neglect this area of investment because something else demands a higher priority. I have routinely worked with individuals who stopped investing in themselves after they got married. Focusing on their spouse or their children seemed natural to them, yet, years after the children moved out, they woke up to find themselves miserable and empty, wondering how they arrived at this place?

The great thing about investing is you can always start. Walking on this journey, we have been laying the groundwork for identity investing. We had to create a safe environment for us to begin tapping into our emotions and to find that unique voice that exists deep inside of us. We need to uncover some of the counterfeit parts of ourselves so we can foster new authentic selves. Once we've tapped into our authentic self, we can begin investing in our true identities, which can yield greater peace and self-acceptance, more satisfying careers, and more meaningful and enjoyable relationships.

Simply put, emotionally-abundant people know who they are—personality traits, strengths and weaknesses, beliefs and values, passions and purpose—and embrace a lifestyle of investing in themselves so they continue to grow and thrive throughout every season of their lives. If you have never taken any time to invest in getting to know yourself more intimately, now is certainly a wonderful time to start.

Discovering Our Personalities

One of the first areas in which we can begin to invest is the area of personality. Many of us have been told things about ourselves throughout our lives, and perhaps we have formed beliefs about who we are—our personalities, our strengths, and weaknesses—that may or may not be true.

For most of my life, I thought I was an extrovert. I was a performer, always on stage in some form or fashion; therefore, I concluded that I must be an extrovert. Still, I could never understand why in large groups I tended to either drift to an empty chair or cling to one person. I could never understand how my other friends could meet a stranger in the grocery line and become friends by the time they checked out at the register. Things that came so easily to them proved to be so difficult for me.

As I came to identify and embrace my more authentic self, I was able to understand my most fundamental personality traits, which dramatically changed the way I began to experience myself. Along my journey, I discovered I am, at the very core, an introvert who can function as an extrovert in certain situations. That was one of the most freeing revelations to me. Knowing I was an introvert allowed me to accept myself and truly understand the qualities God designed in me that He wanted to use. If God needed all of us to be extroverts, He would have just made us all extroverts. He is efficient in that way.

As we begin to explore personality traits, we find many resources that can be both fun and enlightening on our journey. There is no one perfect or conclusive personality inventory or assessment that can universally define us, but each one can yield bits of information that can help us clear away the historic ways we have defined ourselves and open up new possibilities for building Emotional Abundance (EA). Remember, EA is the ability to feel our emotions, to reason through our emotions, to understand our emotions, and to effectively manage our emotions so we can appropriately respond to the people and circumstances around us. We can then experience the greatest amount of peace within.

Psychologists generally look at five basic dimensions of personality—openness, conscientiousness, extroversion, agreeableness, and neuroticism. Because we are all unique, we will all have varying levels of each dimension that make up our core personality. There are online versions of inventories such as the NEO-PI-R that, though not as thorough or conclusive as the tests a psychologist would provide, can provide some clues to our overall personalities along those five dimensions. I often recommend the Meyers-Brigg Personality Inventory, the Keirsey Temperament Sorter, and the Taylor-Johnson Temperament Analysis. Each of those assessments can add helpful information that allow us to create an outline of our basic personality traits.

There are several wonderful books that can help in this phase of your journey as well. I like *The Pathfinder: How to Choose or Change Your Career for a Lifetime of Satisfaction and Success* by Nicholas Lore, *Do What You Are* by Paul D. Tieger and Barbara

Barron-Tieger, *What is the Color of Your Parachute?* by Richard N. Bolles, and *Forty Days to the Work You Love* by Dan Miller and Dave Ramsey.

Taking these inventories is not an attempt to pigeonhole anyone, nor are they tools to identify a certain trait that then becomes an excuse for everything we do or don't do. For those of you who have never come into contact with yourself before this journey, and who do not have a clear concept of who you are at the core, these inventories and assessments can create the outline of your personality in a way you may have never before understood or experienced.

Understanding Our Strengths and Weaknesses

Accordingly, as we uncover and define our core personality traits, we should also explore our strengths and weaknesses as well as our likes and dislikes. Accepting and embracing our authentic selves allows us to look at our weaknesses more easily without needing to run or hide from them.

One of my favorite movies is the romantic comedy, *The Runaway Bride*.[37] If you haven't seen the movie, which you'll find both fun and profound, the story is about a young woman, Maggie, played by Julia Roberts, who has never done much identity-investing. In her attempts at being accepted, she simply becomes whoever her fiancé at the time wants her to be and likes whatever he likes. The biggest problem with this is she never gets to know herself. In the end, she discovers that is what keeps her running away from the altar. Perhaps she unconsciously fears, if she follows through with the marriage, she will lose herself altogether.

---

37 *Runaway Bride* (Warner Bros., 1999).

Even when the *right* man, Graham, who is played by Richard Gere, comes along, she doesn't stop running. The reason she runs is much less about needing to find the right man, and much more about needing to become the *right* woman for herself: a woman who knows who she is, is comfortable with her strengths and weaknesses, and who knows what she likes and doesn't like.

I love the journey this movie follows as Maggie begins to invest in her identity. She cooks eggs in several different ways in order to decide which way she likes her eggs cooked best. She begins to explore her love of industrial lighting fixtures and begins to design them as a hobby and later a career. Along the way, we see a young woman come to life. There is excitement in her eyes. In the end, only after Maggie becomes a whole, complete self is she ready to build a stable relationship with Graham. In true Hollywood fashion, the movie ends with the couple riding off into the sunset on their horses.

Like Maggie, we vitally need to explore and understand our strengths and weaknesses, as well as our likes and dislikes, if we are going to build EA into our lives as individuals and into our relationships. While this exercise may seem trivial, discovering who we are in the small things is as important as discovering who we are in the big things of life. I encourage you to begin exploring your strengths and weaknesses across many facets of life including qualities within your physical self, your emotional self, your spiritual self, your relational self, your financial self, and even your occupational self. Be as specific as possible.

In the same way, I encourage you to begin evaluating your likes and dislikes. As you go through your day, take note of things to which you are drawn or not drawn. Do you love modern art or more classic art? Do you love to watch a good football game on

Sunday afternoon or would you rather curl up with a good book? Do you love suspense movies or romantic comedies? All of those things are clues about what make you uniquely you. Therefore, those things are vital to the concept of EA; that is, being able to manage our emotions well, and holding onto our individuality while being close to someone else who may or may not be exactly like us. How could we do that if we didn't know who we are? We would risk becoming lost in our relationships, much like Maggie became lost in her relationships and only knew to run away from them.

Examining Our Beliefs and Values

Experts have said what you believe (perceive) becomes your reality. You do not believe what you see; rather you see what you already believe. Knowing ourselves requires us to look inside and carefully examine our beliefs and values because they hold the keys to unlocking and creating the reality for which we long.

All of us have an inner system of beliefs and values that we have developed over the course of our lives. They are an accumulation of everything we have experienced in our lives from our parents and families, our religious heritage, our friends and peers, education, work experience, and more. If we take the time to identify what we believe, the things we value and why, we are closer to understanding ourselves at a deeper level and gaining insight into what drives and motivates us.

Beliefs are core convictions we generally hold to be true. Our beliefs grow from what we experience, see, listen to, or reflect upon. They can be spiritual, moral, social, intellectual, financial, or political in nature. From our experiences, opinions are formulated and developed.

Sometimes our beliefs are based on truth and sometimes they are not. Nevertheless, they can have a profound impact on our understanding or misunderstanding of the world around us. If we grew up in an abusive household, we might form the belief that love equals pain. Those of us who didn't grow up with abuse can identify that belief as untrue, but until the abused can recognize that truth and heal from their wounds, that *mis*belief will impact how they experience themselves and everything around them.

As we appraise our beliefs, we can determine their worth or value in our lives; hence values are a natural extension of our core beliefs. Values are traits or qualities that we deem worthwhile. They comprise our top priorities, and our most deeply felt driving forces. Values can include concepts such as equality, honesty, faith, family, education, courage, effort, determination, loyalty, faithfulness, hard work, integrity, responsibility, excellence, respect, teamwork, freedom, beauty, happiness, empathy, wisdom, security, independence, challenge, learning, compassion, discipline, generosity, optimism, innovativeness, and service.

Emotionally-abundant people take the time to understand historic influences in their lives and begin to identify and develop a clear, meaningful set of beliefs and values. Living according to an internal code of values brings meaning, purpose, and direction to our daily lives. Decisions become easier as our understanding of ourselves becomes clearer. Choices are easier and our stress is reduced. Life feels calmer and more stable.

Defining the values that are important to us and comprise our character is fundamental. But doing this work is empty if we do not then engage with our beliefs and values to live them out in our homes, our jobs, and our relationships. Living out our values is one of the most powerful tools we can use to become authentic, centered individuals. The more our choices don't line up with our beliefs and values, the less stability, peace, and happiness we will experience in our lives. The happiest people are those who know what they believe and value and why, and who choose to live their lives and make decisions that both honor and respect their most deeply held principles.

A wise friend once told me, "Lisa, don't listen to what a person says, watch what they *do*. What they *do* will tell you everything about what they believe." What do you believe? Why do you believe it? Do your lifestyle, your choices, attitudes and decisions line up with what you believe? If not, what needs to change?

Identity (including personality traits, strengths and weaknesses, likes and dislikes) lays the groundwork for building a belief system. Our beliefs are prioritized and become our values. Our values inform our attitudes and choices. When everything is congruent, our attitudes and choices will ultimately lead us toward discovering our unique passions and purpose in life.

Nurturing Our Passions and Purpose

What is your passion? What energizes you to get out of bed in the morning? There may be some who say they aren't passionate about anything. I believe we were created to be passionate people. Some of us just haven't invested in our identities enough to recognize what energizes us so we can begin focusing and developing those energies into potential passions.

God did not create us with just one passion. We can experience several different passions over the course of a lifetime, and we can be passionate about more than one thing at a time. There was a season in my life when I was passionate about gardening.

After I had married, I realized I was passionate about cooking though, at the time, I had no knowledge of exactly *how* to cook. I have been pretty consistently passionate about traveling. I am passionate about people.

As I discover a passion and confirm the passion lines up with my personality, my beliefs, and values, I then determine how I need to invest in that passion. If I'm passionate about cooking, what investments am I making? Am I reading cookbooks, taking classes, watching television shows about cooking? You might determine you love reading, coaching, fishing, running, or a million other things. What are you doing to invest in your passions?

Passions can be tricky, though: just because I am passionate about something doesn't necessarily mean that passion is or will become my purpose in life. Could God give us unique passions just to give us gifts and blessings we can enjoy? Investing in our passions creates opportunities for us to connect with God, with ourselves, and with others in ways we couldn't without them. Conversely, not investing in our passions can leave us feeling disconnected, frustrated, depressed, and empty.

Not all of our passions will become our purpose, but our purpose will flow naturally from our passions. In addition, we can experience multiple purposes for our lives as the seasons of life unfold. If we're actively investing in our passions, we will recognize areas along the way that come naturally to us, things to which we are well-suited, where there is a unique talent or ability. However, talent alone will never be enough.

Whatever passion you have must be exercised and disciplined in order to grow into your purpose. I've met many people here in Nashville who are amazing musicians; their talent is stunning. They didn't just wake up one day as extraordinary musicians. They dedicated years, decades even, to studying, practicing, listening to everything they could get their hands on in order to pursue excellence. Somewhere in the process, their passion grew into their purpose.

Being around people who know their identity, who are passionate about connecting with and living out their purpose is exciting. My hope is that investing in your identity will become a continual process in your life. As you embrace the process, you will discover new and wonderful things about yourself, and you will begin to see a significant return on your investment. Live authentically, live passionately, and live in line with your beliefs and values. Now that's a guaranteed investment strategy!

....

Stepping Stones

- Divide a sheet of paper into two columns; one for strengths and one for weaknesses. Begin to identify qualities about yourself in the areas of your physical, emotional, spiritual, relational, financial, and occupational selves, and write them in the columns.

For example, some strengths I might identify are:

- physical – I like my eyes,

- emotional – I like that I am warm and engaging,

- spiritual – I like my consistency and dedication to my faith,

- relational – I like that I am loyal and giving,

- financial – I like that I am not impulsive with spending,

- occupational – I like that I am a hard worker and that I show up.

Your list will have more than one item for each. I didn't even attempt the list for weaknesses because that might be too extensive!

> ***Remember:*** The purpose here is not to create a list that will determine our worth. Our worth is already determined. This is simply an activity to help us arrive at a greater understanding of ourselves, so we can commit to a lifestyle of identity investing.

- Take a moment to affirm each strength and validate the qualities God has designed and built into you that are good. Now take a moment and read through the list of weaknesses. Can you accept yourself even with those weaknesses? Are there any weaknesses you can change or improve? Are those changes realistic?

- Do the same thing with your likes and dislikes. Whereas strengths and weaknesses focus more on internal qualities, likes and dislikes focus more on external preferences. Over the next two weeks, take note of your likes and dislikes, continuing to add to your list.

- Take another sheet of paper and begin to write down your beliefs, again looking at all facets of life. What are the things I believe in most? How did I arrive at those beliefs? Have I simply taken on my parents' beliefs, or have I defined them for myself? Why do I believe what I believe?

- Now take your list of beliefs and narrow them down to a list of your top ten. These are your values. This can be challenging, but if you pair two at a time and determine which one is the most important of the two, narrowing the list will be easier. After you have your top ten list, place those values in order of priority.

- Do your attitudes and choices line up with your values and beliefs? Are there areas of conflict? Write down specifically what needs to change in order for these areas to line up?

- What are your passions? Write a list of activities about which you are passionate. How are you currently investing in those activities? In what areas might you like to begin investing?

- Can you identify areas where a passion could become a purpose? If so, how are you investing in that passion to see if it could become a purpose? If not, continue investing in your passions, keeping an eye open for a purpose that might present itself.

Chapter Eleven

Treating Past Emotional Wounds

Our wounds are often the openings into the best and most beautiful part of us.[38]

—David Richo

At any time during your journey through this book, some difficult emotions from past wounds might have surfaced. Whether they came simply from stopping and quieting yourself in solitude or from the exercises where you began to search for and discover your authentic self, something along the way may have triggered painful feelings, which you may or may not have been aware of for a long time.

If this has been your experience, you are absolutely normal. For so long we have become uniquely adept at pushing our pain to the periphery of our hearts and minds in order to push through and

---

38 David Richo, *The Power of Coincidence* (Boston, MA: Shambala, 2007).

manage the stresses of day-to-day life. We have unconsciously expended a great amount of energy checking out of our emotions and our pain. Now as we are learning to connect with ourselves in a healthy, compassionate way, we are at the same time checking into our emotions and our pain perhaps for the first time. We can expect, normally, that in opening the doorway to feeling, we also open the doorway to painful remnants from past hurts.

We shouldn't avoid the process because avoidance is part of the cycle in which we have been stuck for so long. Wherever *pain points* surface, I believe they create opportunities to dig deeper and experience the most thorough, complete healing possible. Why invest in the extraordinary and challenging work of building peace into our lives only to keep ignoring the pain we buried deep inside? The pain would simply remain a cancer in our interior self that would undermine and weaken the very foundation we have been laboring to build.

For some, awareness of these wounds as they surface and, through processing, journaling, and prayer, healing from these hurts, will be sufficient. For others, these wounds are so painful, perhaps so deep and paralyzing, no amount of processing, reflection, or prayer will prove effective in calming or removing the pain.

If you find yourself at this place, I cannot urge you strongly enough to find a therapist or counselor to walk with you through this season of unpacking and healing. Counseling can be the greatest gift you ever give yourself. Because a therapist doesn't have an emotional or physical history with you, he or she can provide a safe place and an objective perspective for you to begin sharing your story. A therapist can help you uncover your deepest wounds so you can begin healing and unhooking from the people, places, or powers that have enslaved you.

God created us as physical, emotional, and spiritual beings. All three are necessary and important components to understand if we want to build peace into our lives and relationships. At the time we received Christ as our Lord and Savior; He healed us uniquely and completely. Yet, some of our wounds, burdens, and infirmities remain. How can that be? Because as humans living in a fallen world, though we are healed in the spiritual realm, we may not see the fullness or completion of that healing until we reach heaven.

While at the time of conversion, some individuals experience immediate freedom or healing in certain areas, all of us spend our Christian lives *work[ing] out [y]our salvation with fear and trembling.* (Philippians 2:12 NIV) [Additions mine] In other words, we take the salve of God's healing and apply that salve to our physical, spiritual, and emotional wounds so we can find freedom and peace in areas of our lives we never thought possible. If we were all completely healed at the time of conversion, we would all be perfect then, wouldn't we? I find great comfort in hearing Paul describe his affliction in 2 Corinthians 12:7–10 (NIV):

> *...because of these surpassingly great revelations. Therefore, in order to keep me from becoming conceited, I was given a thorn in my flesh, a messenger of Satan, to torment me. Three times I pleaded with the Lord to take it away from me. But he said to me, "My grace is sufficient for you, for my power is made perfect in weakness." Therefore I will boast all the more gladly about my weaknesses, so that Christ's power may rest on me. That is why, for Christ's sake, I delight in weaknesses, in insults, in hardships, in persecutions, in difficulties. For when I am weak, then I am strong.*

I find that so many people who love and pursue God experience an extraordinary amount of emotional shame simply because they haven't gotten *perfect* yet. And when, like I was, they are told that reading the Bible for two weeks will solve all of their problems, and their problems aren't solved at the end of that time, mounds of spiritual shame are heaped on top of the emotional shame of which they are trying to rid themselves.

I wish for the church to be more gentle and compassionate with the weaker, more broken parts of the body so we can experience healing and wholeness, too. Sometimes our wounds are the safest place we know. If the church can create a safe place for the broken to uncover and acknowledge their wounds, we, the body, can begin applying the salve of compassion and understanding. The broken can then start to heal.

As you go through your day, notice your emotional responses to people, stresses, or situations you encounter. Are there times when you leave a conversation wondering why you reacted the way you did? Does anger get triggered easily in you? Do you notice that you have a negative, critical attitude about virtually everything and everyone with whom you interact? Do you always wind up feeling like you are *bad* or *not good enough*?

When something inside you is triggered, take a moment to reflect. These pain points let you know that something inside needs healing and your emotions give you the most direct access to the wound. What are you feeling? What is that emotion about? What are you afraid of? What do you feel guilty about? With whom are you angry?

As you begin to explore, notice what you are feeling and where that feeling manifests in your body. Do you feel tightness across your shoulders? Do you feel a knot in your stomach? Is your heart racing? Just notice these feelings and sensations as they happen. Don't try to push them away. Give yourself permission simply to be in this moment and feel what you are feeling in this moment. Trust that these emotions, like all emotions, will pass. This moment is not the end of your journey.

As memories surface, take note of them. What were the beliefs you formed about yourself, about others, about God based on that memory or experience? Are those beliefs true today? Were you responsible or did you do the best you could? What about others? Were they responsible for what happened to you? Were they acting out in their brokenness in ways that were unacceptable, but the only ways they knew? Where was God? Could He have been right there with you? Could He have wept as you wept, and as you were enraged by the injustice, could He, too, have been enraged by the injustice?

Begin to speak the beliefs about yourself that are true today. In opening yourself to a new belief, in time the negative beliefs will naturally start to unwind themselves and the wound will heal naturally from the inside out. In freeing ourselves from the entanglements of our wounds, we inherently begin to free others from them as well. The effort is not easy. The work is not quick. But as you begin to heal, you will feel awesome!

Stepping Stones

- Set aside an afternoon to have a quiet time and sit with your journal. Pray that God would begin to bring to mind any memories that were painful or traumatic to you and that He would be present as you strive to heal those places inside. Go back as early as you can remember and begin to create a timeline, listing any traumatic experiences that happened to you as a child. How old were you? Where were you when this experience happened? Who was there with you? What was said or done that was wounding to you? What was the worst part of that experience?

- Take a moment to notice any changes that are happening in your body. Are you getting a headache? Is there a tightness across your chest? You don't need to do anything to fix this, just notice and write down what you are experiencing.

- What do you remember thinking or feeling as the experience took place?

- What beliefs did you begin to formulate about others, about God, about yourself from that experience?

- What do you notice thinking or feeling today as you reflect back on those moments?

- Now, taking one experience at a time, simply allow yourself to sit with the wound that resulted from that experience. Don't push the hurt away. Ask God to come and sit with you or hold you as you feel the pain from that wound.

- What are you feeling now?

- What beliefs would you prefer to have about others, about God, about yourself today as you reflect on that experience?

- Begin to breathe deeply and speak out loud the beliefs you've written down. Could those beliefs be true for you today?

- Finish by asking God to continue the healing process in you and to strengthen those new beliefs in you. Please remember that if at any time during this process you feel too unsafe or too painful, now is the time to seek out a counselor who can create a safe place for you to walk through this process.

Chapter Twelve

CHECKING IN – THE INNER JOURNEY

Your vision will become clear only when you can look into your own heart. Who looks outside, dreams; who looks inside, awakes.[39]

—Carl Jung

As we began our journey, I introduced you to a few individuals who were struggling with various issues in their lives. I thought checking in with them and seeing how they have been doing thus far would be a good idea.

39 Quotes.net, STANDS4 LLC, 2015. "Carl Gustav Jung Quotes." Accessed May 1, 2015. http://www.quotes.net/quote/14623.

Kevin and Stacy

Kevin and Stacy first came to see me for couple's therapy. Their marriage was in crisis due to reported communication problems. Stacy felt like Kevin wouldn't communicate with her without screaming; Kevin felt like Stacy was controlling and didn't listen to anything he said. At first Kevin tried to go along with Stacy's demands to avoid conflict, but over time he felt increasingly resentful and bitter. He found himself exploding in anger whenever they would have a disagreement. Stacy, for her part, was unable to see her role in the escalating disputes. She saw Kevin's anger as abusive and came to therapy only to help him deal with his anger management issues.

One day as we began our session, I asked them if they could share what role faith played in their lives. Kevin shared that he was raised in the Baptist church and prayed to receive Jesus into his heart at a senior high school retreat. Once he went away to college however, his church attendance became sporadic and other activities always seemed to take priority. After college, household responsibilities, work, and coaching little league baseball took up most of his weekends. In session, Kevin described his faith as somewhat important to him and an area of his life he would like to explore, if for no other reason than to raise his girls the same way he was raised.

Initially, the only homework I assigned Kevin was self-nurture time, fifteen to twenty minutes per day doing something kind for himself. The first week, Kevin stated that he did a lot more than required. He proudly identified that he spent three to four hours per night watching TV, and that he thoroughly enjoyed *zoning out* as he called that time period. I commended him for his efforts, but politely reminded him that self-nurture time necessitated a quiet space for him to check into his emotions instead of zoning out of them.

After that session, Kevin began to walk around his neighborhood every day before work. He took a few weeks to get over the initial discomfort of not having his headphones playing, but once he did, he noticed that he started thinking about a lot of things he had never thought about before. He started thinking about his day, his life, his relationship with Stacy, even his childhood. I asked him if he ever thought about his faith since that was something he identified as somewhat important to him. I encouraged him to begin thinking about ways he could invest himself in his faith if that were meaningful to him.

Nothing happened at first. He seemed content with his daily walks. However, several weeks later, Kevin shared that he dug in the attic to find his childhood Bible so he could begin reading. He was hesitant to attend church alone, but found a friend at work who would discuss the Bible with him over lunch. Though he sometimes had a hard time understanding a passage he was reading, he stated he felt more peaceful when he read or prayed.

In response to my question on faith, Stacy answered that she was raised Roman Catholic and graduated from a Catholic school, but other than Christmas Eve or Easter, she and her family rarely attended mass. She added she did not find that religion was relevant to her, and she had little interest in addressing faith issues. Though I honored and respected her decision, because my practice is in a church setting, and because faith is an integral part of my work, I encouraged her to think about and remain open to the possible role faith might play in her life.

Two months after that session, Stacy shared that Kevin had asked her to attend church with him and she agreed, though she did so only to make him happy. The church they chose was a non-denominational church close to their home. The service felt totally different from anything Stacy had ever experienced as a child. She liked the music and the casual feel. She especially liked how simply the preacher spoke. Things made sense in a way they had never made sense before. So much so, that at the end of the sermon one Sunday, she found herself praying the prayer the preacher was praying.

Stacy had never felt such peace. She soon found a ladies' Bible study group to help her understand Scripture and mentor her in her newly-found faith. One day, she and I discussed the practice of solitude, which she began to incorporate into her routine. The first several attempts were quite uncomfortable, she informed me in the session. Nevertheless, she was able to experience a sparkling moment or two where she could quiet all of the thoughts, feelings and *to-do's* that bombarded her mind and felt a deep sense of connection and peace with God.

While Kevin and Stacy were each on their own *spiritual* journeys, they were also on their own *emotional* journeys. Early on in our sessions, I noticed that when I asked Kevin how he felt when he and Stacy would argue, he would say something like, "Well, I think she was wrong," or "I just didn't want the girls to hear us fighting." I'd ask again, "How did that make you feel inside?" Again, he offered nothing but a confused glance. I could attempt to fill in the blanks, asking if he felt sad, mad, scared, etc., an emotion he could affirm or deny, yet I understood connecting with his feelings was something entirely foreign to him.

Kevin's dad was a truck driver who was on the road a lot. When his dad was around, he taught Kevin how to do things or fix things out in the garage, but he can never remember his dad sharing a feeling on anything. "We didn't talk about stuff like that," Kevin offered.

Slowly Kevin and I began to build an emotional vocabulary using the emotions chart shown in Chapter Eight. For the first time, when he and Stacy would argue, he could identify what he was feeling in the moment. He could take a time-out to calm his emotions and process through why he was feeling what he was feeling so ultimately he could share his emotions with Stacy.

Emotional honesty was not something that came easily. In the past, his priority was to keep the peace. Passivity was the wall Kevin lived behind in order to keep himself safe, that is, until he'd had enough. Resentment turned into rage that would explode when he least expected to lose control. Once he learned that he could calm his emotions, he no longer needed the passivity to keep him safe, and he could allow himself to be fully present with Stacy, while holding different thoughts, feelings, opinions, and beliefs than she did, without having to abandon himself to her or anyone else.

Kevin noted in session he was starting to feel more comfortable with himself, more real than he had ever felt before. An excitement began to grow as he clarified his beliefs and values, and began to prioritize them. His defined priorities were faith, Stacy, and his children, followed by work, finances, and leisure activities. He desired to be faithful, honest, hard-working, loving, and compassionate. Once those beliefs and values were clarified, he found making decisions based on them easier. Regular church attendance and Bible study became *musts* in his life. He made a decision to turn down some of the overtime he was working so he could spend more time with Stacy and the children. They ate out less, bought some board games to play with the kids, and even planned a weekend alone at home while the kids were at Kevin's parent's house.

Stacy's emotional journey was quite different from Kevin's journey. During the initial stages of therapy, she made many excuses as to why she was never able to find time for self-nurture. In session, any discussion of emotions would make her visibly agitated. The only emotion she was comfortable with was anger, which she readily displayed in session.

Stacy didn't know what to do with the overwhelming feelings of grief she was still experiencing from her mom's death when Stacy was young. Her dad had become isolated and angry, leaving Stacy with no one around her to share what was going on inside. So she shut the door to her emotions. That was easier. Her dad was certainly happier thinking she was all right, which made Stacy feel better, because she was terrified that if she lost her mother, she could lose her dad as well. She could not imagine anything more unbearable.

She never told her dad about the nightmares she was having. Nor did she tell him about her hair-pulling habit. He never asked or noticed, and she never shared.

As Stacy reflected on her teenage years, she realized that after her dad had remarried and moved them to another state, she began to have more of a temper. She didn't like her stepmother, and her dad wasn't around that much, so she rebelled. She talked back, she became very sarcastic, and she spent a lot of time grounded for one reason or another.

We began slowly. Providing a safe place for Stacy to begin telling her story was challenging in and of itself. I encouraged her to begin journaling during this process. She would bring in and read pages from her journal describing memories from her childhood.

One day, as Stacy started to read, tears began to roll down her cheeks. Within a moment or two, she was leaning forward, sobbing uncontrollably with her hands covering her face. I didn't speak and allowed her to experience at that moment exactly what she needed to experience. Several minutes later, her sobs began to soften, and she slowly regained her composure. Afterward, she shared this was the first time she had cried since she was a child.

Amazingly, Stacy felt a huge weight had lifted from her shoulders and though she was exhausted, she felt a deep sense of relief. Over time, as she allowed herself to connect more with her emotions and grieve the loss of her mother, she shared she was less anxious and depressed than she had been in many years.

Though at times she found the process challenging, Stacy was learning how to name and speak all of her feelings – not just the angry ones – and finding that even in anger, she could speak the feeling instead of acting out. That left her feeling tremendously empowered. She was no longer the helpless victim of her emotions; she had the power over them – to feel them, manage them, and calm them. Most importantly, she felt safe.

Letting go of anger became to her a gift, terrifying at some levels because she felt like she was losing a familiar, though counterfeit, friend; freeing because letting go allowed her authentic self to emerge. A more bubbly, relaxed Stacy began to surface.

Her heart for serving in women's ministry continued to grow and not long afterward, she was asked to be a small group leader. The groups she used to avoid, she now loved. She had indeed discovered a new passion among many and is now thinking about returning to school to study theology.

This isn't the end of the story for Kevin and Stacy. They are still on their journey toward building abundance in their lives so they can build abundance in their marriage. They are not perfect and face struggles every step of the way. Still, they have come so far.

Jack

Next, we're going to catch-up with Jack. Jack was fifty-two years old when he first came to my office. He had just been released from the hospital after a suicide attempt. He had struggled with depression for as long as he could remember and simply couldn't take the agony any longer. The pain and emptiness were more than he could bear.

Nothing seemed to work. He had been to countless psychiatrists and had been prescribed just about every kind of anti-depressant. The medication would work for a while, and he would begin to build his hopes that he could live a normal life. Then, just as quickly, the medication would stop working, and he would struggle to get out of bed. The simplest of tasks felt overwhelming.

He was always late for work, couldn't hold a job for more than a couple of months, and was on the verge of filing his second bankruptcy. Jack had been married twice. Both marriages ended in divorce because, as Jack described, "I could never get my act together." His wives had always been critical of him, just like his mom was critical of him growing up.

He was used to the put-downs, the sarcasm, and rage. That's what Mom did to him as a child. She had been diagnosed in recent years with Bipolar Disorder and Borderline Personality Disorder, but growing up he had no definition for the emotional, physical, and verbal chaos he experienced. Nor could he ever plan for or predict the next explosion. Life became solely about survival. Survival came from doing his best to avoid her. Jack summed up his childhood by stating, "we all spent life walking around on eggshells, waiting for the next shoe to drop."

Jack's dad dealt with Mom by staying away. He worked as much overtime as he could just to be away from her. When he was at home, he stayed in the den and did his best not to upset her. Mom ruled with an iron fist, and Dad never said a word. "He never stood up to her to protect us kids," Jack describes, "never stopped her from yelling at us, hitting us, nothing. He just stayed in his den and pretended not to hear."

As an adult, Jack found himself unconsciously attracted to women who were more dominant, like his mom. And like his dad, the more critical and controlling they became, the more passive he became. Now, with his two adult daughters, he has a hard time saying no to their demands, whether they are for money, cars, childcare, or food. He has learned to give them simply what they want so they will be happy and show him the love he has always desired.

From the beginning of our time together, therapy was a slow process. Feeling safe took him several months. A simple question could be followed by many moments of silence and a confused response of "I don't know." Jack repeatedly broke down because he didn't know what he thought, didn't have a clue as to what he felt, and experienced such a deep sense of worthlessness and shame that he was consumed.

The only time he engaged initially was when I asked him what role faith played in his life. "Oh," he offered, "my faith is the most important thing in my life. Growing up we went to church every Sunday and Wednesday. That was the only thing I could count on." Since becoming a Christian in junior high school, he has attended Sunday services and a men's Bible study regularly. "It is something for me to hold onto. It gives me hope," he shared.

His hope though, at times, seemed clouded by shame. Jack couldn't understand why, since he had become a Christian and had been prayed over again and again, he had not been healed of his depression. He would listen to the sermons, he would believe what the preacher taught, but for some reason, what seemed to work for everyone else around him didn't seem to work for him. His Bible study leader had met to pray with him several times, but had grown weary. He told

Jack he needed to get into the Word and get over his issues, believing they were simply a matter of faith.

My initial encouragement was for Jack to begin to practice solitude. However, I wanted him to engage in the process only if solitude felt meaningful to him, and to end the time when the practice stopped being meaningful. I wanted his focus to be simply on enjoying the experience and not another requirement that, if he failed, would bring him more condemnation and shame.

In session, he would talk about spirituality quite often. Certainly he believed wholeheartedly, but just as certainly, his most deeply-held beliefs about God seemed eerily similar to his beliefs about his mother. He was conflicted because, though he knew in his mind that God was good, loving, and kind, he often experienced God as punitive, unpredictable, and unmerciful.

Jack's spiritual journey overlapped significantly with his emotional journey. As we introduced self-nurture into our work, he found the practice difficult, because as Jack described, "Everything I did just ended up making me feel like a total failure. I couldn't even get the concept of being kind to myself right." He was so terrified of failing and the shame he perceived that failure would bring, even answering a question could leave him in tears.

Little by little, Jack found he didn't need to have all the answers. He slowly began to give himself permission to fail and trust he could still be okay. As he learned how to recognize the negative thoughts that tormented him daily, he was able to speak more balanced and kind thoughts to himself. His demeanor changed dramatically over time. Where he once appeared fragile, his body almost shaking, he began to exude more calm. When I would ask him what he thought or felt, he could look me in the eye and tell me without equivocating.

Every step was new territory for Jack. Nothing came naturally because of his experiences from his childhood. Yet Jack was able to cultivate new skills that changed how he experienced just about everything in his life—from being kind to himself, from connecting with his thoughts and emotions, to allowing his authentic self to emerge so he could discover and build a solid, strong identity. None of those things would have been possible without healing the deep emotional wounds that had festered in so much of his life in the past. Every step of healing yielded a new place of freedom that could grow.

And grow he did. Once Jack could see his mom had been ill and could not give him the love and acceptance every child deserves, he could begin to forgive her. He could unhook from the destructive beliefs he held about himself and create more balanced, truthful, kind beliefs about who he was as a person.

What's even more amazing is, over time, the more Jack was able to speak to himself with kindness and compassion, the more he began to experience God as kind and compassionate.

Only then could he be prepared to move forward on his journey and learn how to experience others in a similar way.

Once again, consider the example of our tree – EA begins deep down in our roots, in our relationship with God, and moves up into our relationship with ourselves. When we experience and cultivate EA from the roots up, we can begin to discover and nurture true EA and peace in our relationships. But we'll tackle that a little bit later.

Debra

The last individual we will revisit is Debra. Debra was forty-eight years old when she pursued therapy in order to deal with her addiction to alcohol. Our initial conversation revealed that Debra grew up in an alcoholic family. She was the oldest of four children.

Growing up, she watched daily as her father came home from work and began his evening ritual of pouring himself a few drinks before dinner. With each drink, his agitation increased. He would start with angry comments about the news. Then he would bicker with her mom, and yell at the kids to, "shut up so I can have some peace and quiet," as Debra recalled. By suppertime, he was in a virtual rage. His bickering escalated into cursing and name-calling. Seemingly he was looking for something that would give him an excuse to explode.

Debra remembered a night when she was six years old that her dad stood up from the table and began to beat her mom violently. Debra immediately took the little ones to their room. When she came back to the dining room, she started pulling on her dad's arm, desperately trying to get him off of her mom. He merely flung her off while he continued his vicious attack.

One night when Debra was fifteen years old, as another fight began, she stood in front of her mom with a knife and threatened to kill her dad if he ever touched her mom again. He never did.

To make matters worse, Debra was molested by a teacher when she was twelve years old. Though she told her parents, they didn't believe her and refused to take any action that might embarrass the family.

Since then, Debra has always found herself in relationships where there is a lot of drama. Whether the drama is from her boyfriend's ex-girlfriend, his boss, or a nosy neighbor, there is always a fight to be had, and she is ready for battle. The relationships usually end when there are no more battles to wage.

The losses have been tremendous for Debra. She began to rely on alcohol many years ago as a way to deal with the pain of the break-ups. She feels so alone, and the sadness is overwhelming. She just wants to feel loved, to feel safe. Her current boyfriend truly does love her but can't take Debra's drama anymore.

When I asked what role faith played in her life, she responded she had a general belief in God. She related having a lot of anger toward Him, not understanding how a loving God could have allowed her to experience everything she did as a child. She also felt God had abandoned her just like her parents did when she told them of her molestation. Certainly she could not feel safe with someone else who was going to leave.

Debra's spiritual healing would come later, as a natural extension of her emotional healing. Her emotional wounds were more important than any other goal, at least initially. Debra needed to grieve. She needed to unpack and sort through all the traumas from childhood that impacted her life.

At the same time, we began to implement self-nurture. I encouraged her to begin writing her story in her journal. One day, as she began to read from her journal, she looked up in despair and asked where God was in all of this. I asked if she could see Him in any of her memories. "If He was there, where would He have been?" I pondered.

Though her initial reaction was one of anger, that God indeed had never been there, over time she began to soften. She was able to see the possibility that God was there with her. She could believe God was not the cause of her child-hood experience, nor could He have prevented broken people from doing broken and terrible things.

From that point on as she read, she would imagine God in His white robe, holding her in His lap as they rocked in a rocking chair. She was comforted to imagine Him holding her, crying with her, saddened by all she had to endure.

Over time, she recognized as she called to mind a painful memory from her childhood, though she could see what had happened, the event felt much more distant. Now instead of being lost in the memory and consumed with the pain, the memory was there, but hazier somehow. What once brought tremendous pain only surfaced as a mild sadness, nothing more.

Steadily, as Debra grieved and learned to connect with her emotions in a healthy way, she could name them, calm them, and manage them appropriately. She learned to recognize people and situations that would trigger her protective instinct or her need for vindication. Instead of reacting out of those emotions, she could stop herself, calm herself, and decide the healthiest option for dealing with the situation at hand.

Although different from anything Debra had ever known, she felt good. She felt healthy, which gave her continued motivation for her journey. As we began to discuss the concept of authenticity and her identity as God's beloved, all of the criticisms and lies spoken by her father flooded her mind. This time, however, she was able to recognize the lies and speak the truth to herself. She was on the verge of discovering her belovedness and her worth.

As Debra continued to understand her true identity and invest in herself, she found strengths that she had never before been aware of, such as her tender heart for others, her creativity, and her loyalty. In defining her values and beliefs, she realized her faith was more important to her now than ever before, and she wanted to get closer to God. He felt safer now, not so cold or distant. She began to attend church and invited Christ into her heart.

As she studied and grew more in her faith, she wanted her life to reflect her faith. Learning about God's covenant of marriage, she and her boyfriend decided to meet with the pastor and get married. A fancy wedding wasn't nearly as important as living consistently with her beliefs and values. All of a sudden, the marriage license seemed to be a whole lot more than just a simple piece of paper.

Debra's journey certainly hasn't been quick or easy, but the peace and joy she is experiencing as a result of her diligence is paying off. The next step on Kevin's, Stacy's, Jack's, and Debra's individual journeys is to take the healing, the skills, the peace they have found in their relationship with God and themselves, and bring that peace into their relationships with others. In building a strong, solid foundation, we create the necessary environment to build strong, solid relationships.

SECTION III

Peace with Others

SECTION III

INTRODUCTION

Each friend represents a world in us, a world possibly not born until they arrive, and it is only by this meeting that a new world is born.[40]

—Anais Nin

The Gift of Spring

As I sit down to write this morning, my eyes are continually drawn outside my window to witness the miracle happening before me. Spring is here, and everywhere little buds of green are pushing their way up from the ground's surface. The forsythia's yellow blossoms are beginning to explode, and tiny red petals are filling the barren branches of my beloved rose bushes. Before long, tulips in every color of the rainbow will begin to steal the show as they announce their arrival with an unequaled majesty.

In amazement, I wonder how this happened. Yesterday everything was dead and brown, yet today the whole world is being

---

40 Anais Nin, *The Diary Of Anais Nin, Vol. 2 (1934-1939)*(FL: Harcourt, Brace & Company, 1967).

reborn before my very eyes. Spring is my favorite time of year.

A couple of years ago, my husband and I planted some Leyland cypress trees in our yard. Ever since, we have been faithfully watering them and fertilizing them exactly the way we were instructed, yet they have not grown quickly to become the grand towers of shade I had envisioned.

So a few weeks ago when a lawncare specialist was spraying the lawn, I inquired as to why my trees weren't growing like they should. The man chuckled and began to explain that the trees were indeed growing, but most of their growth thus far was underneath the surface of the ground. He described that during the first two years or so, the trees were establishing a healthy root system and that they needed to grow big underground before they started to grow big above ground. He encouraged me to be patient, knowing they would eventually take off and grow bigger than I could imagine.

Cultivating New LIFE in Our Relationships

At that moment, everything made sense. This new life, these new beginnings on display in my garden are a reflection of where we are on our journey toward cultivating new life and new abundance in our relationships. All of the work we have done thus far has been in establishing and growing our root system underground, so we could have a strong, solid trunk. Now, the final stage is being set to see the healthy new growth reach far and wide into our relationships.

Everything before has been in preparation for this moment. Now we are ready to see and experience the fruits of our labor. We could not have worked backward. We could never experience the beauty of a healthy, peaceful relationship with anyone else if we had neglected to build Emotional Abundance (EA) into our relationships with God and ourselves. We defined EA earlier as the ability to feel our emotions, to reason through our emotions, to understand our emotions, and to effectively manage our emotions so we can appropriately respond to the people and circumstances around us.

All of the unhealthiness that we bring with us from our past contaminates the experiences and relationships in our present. We learn as children what relationships look like primarily from the adults around us. We may or may not have had an understanding of whether what we were seeing then was healthy or unhealthy. So for most of us, as we enter into and build adult relationships, we do what we've seen done before; we build the house that we've seen built before. When our efforts don't work or we don't get the results we'd like, we're left wondering what to do next.

We find the problems we encounter in one relationship seem to follow us into all of our relationships. We build defenses. We are hesitant to trust because everything before has taught us there isn't any place or any person where we are safe to relax and let down our guards, much less provide the genuine acceptance and love our hearts desire.

Many of us simply place the blame for our unhealthy or unsuccessful relationships squarely on the other person's back and move on. In a throw-away society, relationships haven't fared much better than our appliances, our water bottles, or our cars. Nothing is made to last, and when we're done with something or it breaks, instead of fixing the item, we simply throw it away and get another.

However, in doing so, do we lose a powerful opportunity to learn and grow? Whether we've experienced the pain of losing an unhealthy relationship or simply remain stuck and miserable in one, beginning again is never too late. We can always start healing, learning, and growing so we can cultivate EA into our relationships.

If we have been diligent to study the first two sections of this book, we are hopefully more aware and more capable of understanding our wounds and healing them so we can start learning how to build *LIFE* into our relationships.

LIFE stands for:
LIVING calmly, connected, and centered
IMPLEMENTING healthy communication
FREEING others as I free myself
ENGAGING collaborative conflict-resolution skills

The first step toward building *LIFE* into our relationships begins with us. While we cannot change those around us, we are powerful enough to change how we choose to engage our relationship partners. Our job is first and foremost to *Live* calmly, connected, and centered. In learning how to manage our emotions, we become less easily triggered, our emotions less impacted by the people and situations that surround us. We need to remain calm if we are to connect with our thoughts, feelings, beliefs, and values in a meaningful way.

Learning to live calmly, connected, and centered creates balance and prepares us to *Implement* healthy communication. Healthy communication creates emotional honesty with those around us by allowing us to speak what we are thinking and feeling in a healthy, respectful way.

I cannot speak for another, I can only speak for myself by using I-statements that allow others to know and understand my emotional experience; e.g., "When I didn't get the promotion at work, I felt disappointed and angry." I own responsibility for my experience, yet I can allow others to know where I am, emotionally speaking, the more I am willing and able to share with them.

In order to build health into our relationships, we must begin to *Free* others as we free ourselves. Though speaking what we are thinking and feeling in a healthy, respectful way is good, we can never force or control someone's response. We choose to speak our thoughts and feelings simply because doing so is a requirement for us to be healthy individuals. If we are only willing to speak if we can guarantee a certain outcome or response, we are being manipulative. EA will never be gained from manipulation.

The very definition of emotional differentiation is that ability to hold onto myself, my identity, my thoughts and feelings, my beliefs and values while being close to someone who may or may not be exactly like me. I build EA the more I allow myself to hold onto the things that make me uniquely me without abandoning those things to another person's identity or preferences. But differentiation also means that I allow others to hold onto themselves at the same time and cultivate their own identity, values, and beliefs without requiring them to abandon themselves to me.

Sometimes no matter how hard we work, or how much we try, we will find ourselves in conflict with someone we love or care about—a veritable certainty for any human being. Even in the healthiest sense, we are carrying our unique selves into the world and are constantly brushing up against (or bumping into) others who are carrying around their unique selves. At some point, there will be some friction or bruising from these interactions.

The goal should not be to learn how to avoid every conflict, but to learn how to work through a conflict while preserving as much health and peace as possible, both individually and in the relationship. Therefore, the final step toward building *LIFE* into our relationships is to *Engage* collaborative conflict-resolution skills.

Carrying all of the principles we have been acquiring into any conflict resolution is important for us. We must do our own work ahead of time to process our thoughts and feelings, and be calm, connected, and centered if we are to enter into a discussion with anyone. This enables us to then create a calm, compassionate, cooperative environment for both parties to share and resolve disagreements.

For most of my life, when dealing with conflict, I would pray that disagreements would go away or be resolved quickly. I looked to the removal of the problem as the sign of growth. More recently though, as I have walked farther along my journey, my focus has begun to shift. Now instead of seeing the destination (the resolution of the problem) as the sign of growth, I have begun to see the journey itself as the process *for* my growth. In doing this, my goal is no longer to get past the conflict, but rather to walk through the conflict well, whatever the conclusion may be.

If *walking well* is our focus, we will find ourselves encountering more peace than we could have ever imagined. We will be able to look up and enjoy the beauty of relationships the way God intended. We will experience increased stability from decreased drama in every aspect of our lives and we will be empowering the children in our lives to see what abundant relationships look like so they can build abundant relationships both as children today and also later as adults. Thus, what one person in a family is willing to do in order to cultivate EA for themselves can have ripple effects that can spread peace far and wide for generations to come.

Chapter Thirteen

LIVING CALMLY, CONNECTED, AND CENTERED

The cyclone derives its powers from a calm center. So does a person. [41]
—Norman Vincent Peale

In Section II, we embarked on an inner journey, learning to look inside ourselves to find the essence of our healing. Much of what we discussed centered around increasing our levels of Emotional Abundance by learning to calm or manage our emotions internally and by aligning our emotional pipes so we can stay consistently connected with what we are thinking and feeling. Over time, a powerful force begins to swell deep inside our being, a centrifugal force, where our energies are concentrated and grounded. We as individuals are becoming physically, emotionally, and spiritually strong.

---

41 Norman Vincent Peale, *http://izquotes.com/quote/300387.*

Our journey toward peace in our relationships takes these same principles and begins to apply the steps to our exterior life in our relationships. Emotional Abundance (EA) – the ability to effectively manage our emotions so we can appropriately respond to the people and circumstances around us – doesn't allow us to exist in a vacuum. All of us, at some point, must come into contact with others. As Gaius Davies conveys about John Bunyon's beliefs regarding our journey here on earth, "First, the journey is above all an inward and spiritual toil; the outward aspects only secondary....[yet our] pilgrimage always has to do with relationships."[42]

From the time we open our eyes in the morning, we are constantly coming into contact with people – whether they share our bed, our house, our neighborhood, our office, or our church. At the point we make contact, something unique happens. A spark ignites, a reciprocity of energy is exchanged, and a dynamic is created.

Our best understanding of relational dynamics comes from the system of dynamics set up in our family of origin. The family style where we were raised carries a powerful force where individual members learn to connect with one another in unique ways that are mutually affecting. Patterns evolve whereby each member adopts a certain role within the family that allows the system to function as a whole.

Family systems form the basis for all our human interactions and relationships because the role we adopt within the family system is usually carried into all of our future adult relationships. These roles become a stable, though sometimes unconscious, part of our identity. Because family systems are driven by a process

42 Gaius Davies, *Genius, Grief & Grace: A Doctor Looks at Suffering & Success* (Scotland, UK: Christian Focus Publications, 2001) 86-87.

called homeostasis, the tendency to maintain stability or equilibrium, they are therefore usually resistant to change.

Have you ever had the experience of going back home to visit after having been away and feeling as though you were fifteen years old again the moment you walked through the door? That is the power of homeostasis at work within the family system. Some people might resist returning home because of the incredibly strong dynamics that leave them feeling child-like, helpless, weak, or even angry. Avoiding home may seem to provide the best solution.

While there are some extreme situations where home was physically, emotionally, or sexually abusive, and being cut-off provides the option of last resort for survival and health, most of us experience the fullness of our relational healing by returning home, figuratively speaking. This means our healing becomes complete the more we can understand our role in the family system, learn how to unhook from the homeostatic force that wants us to stay the same, and begin to differentiate ourselves well enough to interact with others, even our family of origin, from a place of peace and EA. The power of returning home frees us from our historical role in the family system and allows us to carry this freedom – this new, solid self into all of our adult relationships.

Interestingly, we can at any time, from any place, with any person begin to exercise EA in our relationships. No decision for EA is ever wasted. The muscles we strengthen in one relationship can be translated into other relationships. Please note, the goal is never to change or fix someone else. The goal is to heal, understand, and grow ourselves so we can engage in any relationship and experience peace for ourselves as we connect with our loved ones.

Living Calmly, Connected and Centered

When I come into contact with anyone and that exchange of energy takes place, I have one of two choices: either I unconsciously react to the other's energy; or I can choose to recognize what's going on inside of me, calm myself in the moment so I can better understand my emotions, and determine how I would best like to respond to the other person.

Several years ago, I had a friend who would constantly confront me about certain issues or concerns she had with me. Because of my individual history, my initial internal default was usually one of *I need to be good, I need to please everyone around me, I need them to like me.* So when she would approach me, my reaction was one of intense anxiety, and I would experience an implosion of sorts. I felt such shame that, without having learned to keep myself calm and connected to think through whether there was any validity to her comments, I would just break down and own responsibility for whatever she was saying. I would promise to do better so I could once again feel that I was good, that she was pleased with me, and that I was okay.

Later in the relationship, as I was on my healing journey, I found when she would confront me, I didn't automatically have to panic. I learned I could calm myself and keep myself safe. I was no longer held captive to the drive to be good, to be pleasing, or to be liked, which allowed me to stay fully present with my friend as well as connected myself. I could think through things and recognize inside whether there was anything I needed to own or not more easily. Then I could respond to her without abandoning myself in the process.

Each of us has defense mechanisms we learned long ago in our families of origin. When confronted by a friend or loved one, some individuals instinctively become angry and aggressive. Some shut down completely. Others use sarcasm to deflect criticism or project blame to shift the focus of the conversation. No matter what your defense mechanisms are, they are your unconscious attempts to keep yourself safe. If you say, "This is just the way I am," you certainly will never grow, and you will be destined to carry the same pattern into every relationship for the rest of your life. There are better ways you can learn to keep yourself safe.

Learning the Art of Calm

When we are not calm and our emotions escalate, our brains become flooded with the same stress hormones that are activated in *fight or flight* situations, making processing information clearly more difficult. We cannot rationally think through the message or the response we would like to give; therefore, our reactions become more emotionally-charged impulses rather than thought-filled responses.

In order to avoid becoming emotionally charged and hypersensitive, we need to become aware of situations that trigger these emotional impulses in us. In those moments, we must develop our emotional tool belt by learning how to calm ourselves right in the moment. Sometimes when we are just starting out, we need to take a time-out so we can get away by ourselves and soothe ourselves, but the goal is never to use the time-out as a means of avoidance or escape. The goal should always be to reconnect from a place of calm so we can engage with our thoughts and construct a healthy, meaningful response.

One way to help build calm into our overall lives is to learn the deep-breathing exercises from Chapter Six. Just to restate, we breathe in and out like we are breathing through a straw, from deep in our bellies. We should be able to feel our stomach and lower back expanding and contracting if we are breathing properly. Our shoulders should be relaxed. Once we get going, we begin to slowly count to three, hold for three, and exhale for three. Then increase the breath to a four-count, then a five-count. The goal is to physiologically slow down our breathing, which helps lead the body into a state of calm.

Another way to help build calm into our lives is to use guided imagery to further reinforce our deep breathing. When we are breathing, we can close our eyes and begin to imagine the calmest, safest place on earth. For me, having grown up in Florida, my calm, safe place is the beach. This place can be anywhere, but usually somewhere in nature is best, a place that cannot be intruded upon by outside elements such as people or technology.

As we breathe, we can begin to put ourselves into our calm, safe place, imagining what makes our haven so special for us. For me, as I place myself on the beach, I can feel the warmth of the sun on my skin, I can hear the seagulls as they fly above, and feel the rhythm of the waves gently crashing against the shore. The sand is warm against my skin, and I can smell the salt-permeated air. We should make our calm, safe place as specific as possible and engage as many of our senses as we can so, in moments of intense emotion, we can go to that place and use that visualization to help us calm ourselves in the here and now.

Muscle relaxation is yet another tool that can help us manage our emotions and our physiological stress state. When doing relaxation exercises, begin by isolating one muscle group at a time, tensing the area for five to ten seconds and then releasing. Then move on to the next muscle group until all of your muscles have been relaxed. Begin with the facial muscles, then the hands, lower forearms, upper forearms, shoulders, upper back, lower back, chest, stomach, hips and buttocks, thighs, calves, and feet. Once you've completed a set, if you find any remaining tension in any muscle groups, do a second or third set.

With all of these exercises, you may need to take a time-out initially in a discussion, in order to implement them and soothe yourself enough to re-engage the conversation. Hopefully over time though, as you get better at them, you will become more in tune with your anxiety level and do the exercises almost instantaneously, without having to take a time-out.

Staying Connected with Myself

I've been in many conversations with loved ones where I could feel my emotions getting out of hand. Before I could exert control, my mind was racing, my thoughts were scattered, and my message echoed a volume of words that said little. I was left to hurl accusations in a desperate attempt to be heard and to keep myself safe. Nothing productive is ever accomplished in conversations where my emotional stress disconnects me from myself.

In that emotional state, I cannot formulate a coherent thought or message, therefore I am left conveying only intense emotions in an attempt to create safety for myself. As I learn to calm myself, I find I am better able to remain connected to myself, understand why I am feeling what I am feeling, and learn how to communicate my message clearly to my loved one.

Even more, remaining calm allows me to remain connected to my deepest self, my spiritual and emotional identity, my values and beliefs, and communicate in a way that is congruent with who I am. An individual who claims great spiritual and emotional maturity yet consistently spews forth anger, judgment, and condemnation at others reveals his utter incongruity. EA is never incongruent. Therefore, remaining connected and calm so my words and my actions reflect accurately who I am in my most authentic self is essential.

Connection with myself allows me to stay in a constant position of listening inwardly to my internal reactions and responses to those around me. This self-awareness is vital if I desire to connect with others in their emotion without absorbing their emotion into mine. If I am tuned into my emotions, I can be present with my friend's anger, frustration, or sadness without having to become angry, frustrated, or sad myself. As I learn to hold onto myself well—my identity, my thoughts and feelings, my beliefs and values—I begin to carry my own emotional weight. Doing this frees me to be more present with loved ones, as well as more compassionate with whatever they are going through, without their emotions, or their issues, becoming mine.

Building Safety, Openness, Respect, and Compassion Into Our Relationships

I have learned I no longer need anyone (humanly speaking) to make me safe—I am safe. I am okay. The result of my confidence in my inner self is I can create an environment that is safe for two people to exist in relationship. This is not a job or responsibility, simply a byproduct of the peace that is growing inside of me.

Amazingly, the more I am able to keep myself safe, the more I am able to open myself to those with whom I am in relationship. Sometimes, unconsciously, I close myself off from allowing others to know the real, authentic me. I learned to build walls earlier in life because I knew no other way to keep myself safe. Now that I have learned how to care for myself abundantly, I can open the door of my authentic self to others, and allow myself to encounter their authentic selves as well. Simply put, I am able to come face to face with one of my own species and feel safe enough to enjoy the experience.

Living centered also allows me to hold respect for myself and others in relationship. *Respect* means to hold esteem or regard for someone; to show consideration. Yet for many, the definition of respect has changed somewhat over the years. Respect has come to mean if you give me whatever I want, I will respect you or think you are all right. The notion implies that you must respect me before I will respect you. You must show consideration for me before I will show consideration for you; therefore, you have the job of creating a safe environment for me and if you do that, I will do the same for you.

Respect, in the truest sense, is actually the opposite. I respect others because I have respected myself first. I don't require respect from another. Let me repeat—I don't require respect from another. I create an environment of respect because I am a person of respect. I am therefore able to esteem another or show regard for them.

If a person is consistently disrespectful to me, however, I don't have to allow myself to be perpetually abused in order to be respectful. As a healthy individual who respects herself, I might simply have to speak my concerns and perhaps learn to draw healthier boundaries in order to maintain respect for myself and another in the relationship. We will dig more into the concept of boundaries later.

As safety allows openness to flourish and openness allows respect to flourish, respect then creates a space where compassion can grow vibrantly and bountifully. If a relationship were to be described as a flower, compassion would be the very tip of the petals. The most beautiful moments in the flower's bloom are when the petals are fully open, fully extended, as if the bloom is reaching toward the heavens. The longer we are calm, connected, and centered, the more we can allow ourselves to fully bloom and experience safety, openness, respect, and ultimately compassion for another.

Compassion means to be aware of and show sympathy or concern for another's suffering. Like everything we've discussed before, compassion is a gift that must be given to ourselves first. How well do I show compassion to myself in my own woundedness? How kind and concerned am I toward the weaker parts of me? For many, the answer would be we are not very kind or compassionate with ourselves. Yet, the more compassion I am able to give myself, the more I am able to speak kindly to myself, the more I am able to offer compassion as a gift to my relationships. That those of us who are the most condemning and critical of ourselves are usually the most condemning and critical of others as well is no wonder. Compassion and condemnation cannot co-exist in the same space.

This stage of the journey is about taking the EA we discovered in our relationship with ourselves and carrying that into all of our relationships. Like everything else we've discussed, bringing ourselves wholly to other relationships is also a process. Success is not measured by one experience. Success is simply derived from what we have learned from each experience that carries us further on our journey toward abundance. Even our failures are not wasted if we are able to learn from them. Relationships simply become the training ground for us to continue healing, continue growing, and continue building EA and peace into every aspect of our lives.

....

Stepping Stones

- Begin today to become more mindful or aware of your anxiety level when you are with other people. Do you feel calm? Are there moments when you can feel your body start to tense? Journal about these experiences. If your anxiety spikes, what happened that caused the spike? What is that emotion about for you?

- Practice daily the art of calming exercises to begin to strengthen your emotional tool-belt. Practice using some of the tools even when you are with others.

- When you are with someone else, notice what you are thinking and feeling during the conversation. Become aware of what you are feeling in your body and where the feeling manifests itself.

- As you become aware of what you are thinking and feeling, begin to think about how you would like to respond. What is the message you would like to convey? Are you simply emotionally reacting to the person, or are you able to share a calm, thoughtful response?

- Begin to think about the aspects of safety, openness, respect, and compassion in regards to your relationships with others. When you are with others, notice how safe you feel. Do you need others to make a place or situation safe for you? Could you possibly keep yourself safe?

- How open are you with others – do you allow others to experience your authentic self or do you hide safely behind your defenses? Write down some of your defense defaults.

- Consider how much respect is created in your relationships. Do you create an environment of respect? If not, how can you begin to increase your respect for yourself and others?

- Are you a compassionate person? Do you tend to be critical and judging of others – of yourself? How can you begin today to speak more kindly to yourself? Write down some ways you could offer compassion to yourself and those around you.

Chapter Fourteen

Implementing Healthy Communication

The single biggest problem with communication is the illusion that it has taken place.[43]

—William Hollingsworth Whyte

Rick and Audrey

Several years ago I was working with a middle-aged couple, Rick and Audrey, who had been married for fifteen years. As I questioned Audrey to learn more about what wasn't working in their relationship, she openly shared her frustration with Rick. From her perspective, he just wasn't willing to meet her needs. Her primary complaints were Rick's lack of affection and lack of help around the house. I followed up by asking what she had done previously to address her concerns with Rick. She replied she had

---

43 William Hollingsworth Whyte, "Is Anybody Listening?," *Fortune*, September 1950, 174.

told him repeatedly he was selfish and didn't care about her at all.

Rick for his part, was mostly silent during my initial conversation with Audrey. He seemed frustrated and angry just hearing her complaints. When I addressed him to find out his concerns, his only response was, "Her." He described himself as attentive. He didn't go out with his buddies to drink. He just didn't know what her problem was. "I think when she gets like this, she's just crazy," he explained. "I should have known she'd be just like her mother. This really has nothing to do with me. I'm just here to get her the help she needs."

I asked Audrey if she had ever shared with Rick her specific complaints and how she felt about them. She replied he should know. "If he loves me, he should know the things that are important to me and should try to meet my needs."

While I understood Audrey's perspective and her frustration with the dynamic at work between the two of them, thinking that Rick was able to somehow *know* what her needs were if she was not able to communicate them clearly was a stretch.

To be honest, most of us at some point have had the experience of expecting or assuming someone should know something about us even though we have never communicated our thoughts or feelings to them. So often we carry hurts and frustrations regarding unmet needs that we have never spoken.

This illustration shows, among other things, how poorly Rick and Audrey communicate with one another. In her attempt at communicating, Audrey accuses Rick of being selfish, of not loving her or trying to meet her needs. Rick feels defensive and lashes back by placing the blame on Audrey, calling her names, and belittling both her and her mother. None of this communication is healthy and none of their interactions will bring Emotional

Abundance (EA)–being able to effectively manage our emotions so we can appropriately respond to the people and circumstances around us–to the relationship.

Implementing Healthy Communication

Communication is the exchange of thoughts, feelings, opinions, or ideas through speaking, writing, symbols, or behavior. In order to have effective communication, we first have to connect with our thoughts, feelings, opinions, or ideas; then we must formulate the message we want to send.

Communication works a lot like cell phones do. When we communicate our thoughts and feelings to a partner or friend, we are pinging our emotional coordinates to them, much like a cell phone pings its geographic coordinates to a cell phone tower.

Cell phones continually transmit radio signals to nearby cell phone towers. When a signal is transmitted, a *ping* is sent to the tower with information that can be stored as to the location of the cell phone, any calls made, dates, times, etc. There have been many instances where emergency services or law enforcement have used the *pinged* information to rescue lost individuals or track persons of interest.

In much the same way, we human beings use communication to send emotional signals to those with whom we are in a relationship. The messages I send are *pinged* to my loved one. They *ping* messages back to me. However, if I am unwilling to share my emotional coordinates with my partner, how would they ever know where I was, emotionally speaking, much less how to find me?

The answer is, they wouldn't. They would simply be left to guess where I was or assume where I could be found. In ideal communication, there would be a constant flow of pinging, back and forth. I ping to my husband where I am emotionally, and he pings back to me where he is emotionally. I ping again to him, and he pings again to me. Throughout the dialog, there is an openness, a natural curiosity to hear more, learn more, and perhaps understand more about my partner than I knew previously. I also have an opportunity to share myself safely and respectfully with my partner.

Speaking Only For Myself

Being *willing* to communicate is the first step toward building EA in our relationships. Equally important is that we learn *how* to communicate. There are distinctive components that will improve the overall effectiveness of our communication and increase the likelihood the message we want to send is precisely the message we do send. The first component of healthy communication is learning how to speak for ourselves and only ourselves. I can never speak for another, especially if that person is the partner or friend with whom I am speaking. They have their unique personality, history, and emotional wounds that create the lens through which they experience life. They own and define their experiences and self. Mine is the only experience that I can own and communicate if I am attempting to develop healthy communication.

Once I have done the necessary prep work to understand and clarify what I am thinking and feeling, I can begin respectfully speaking them to others using *I-statements*. I-statements are messages that keep the focus of my communication on exactly that—me. Again, my energies should be centrifugal, resonating internally with my identity, my experiences, my beliefs, and my values.

When the focus of my communication remains on me, my partner or friend can sit more safely with me and has the best chance of listening and understanding the message I am trying to send. If the focus of my communication is on the other person and what their words or behaviors have done to affect me negatively, then that person cannot sit safely with me. Their defenses go up and their focus shifts from trying to understand me to trying to defend themselves in order to keep themselves safe—a natural instinct.

If they respond defensively to me, the chances are higher that I am going to respond back defensively, and the conversation will begin to escalate into a conflict I never wanted or intended. Therefore, if my primary mode of communication is one of using *You-statements*, I'm probably never going to be heard, and I'm going to remain trapped in a cycle of intermittent explosions that never get resolved.

When learning how to implement *I-statements*, I recommend beginning with the following format: "When _____ happened, I felt _____(refer to the emotions chart in Chapter Eight and be specific), and I just wanted to share that with you."

First of all, the initial statement "When _____ happened"—is the incident that caused the distress. For example, "When the car got wrecked last week," "When I didn't learn about the boat purchase until it was sitting in the driveway," or "When I sat waiting at the restaurant for an hour"—those are all ways to share what we are thinking and feeling using *I-statements*.

You-statements, on the other hand, tend to focus on the other person: "When you totaled the car last week," "When you bought a boat without having ever discussed it with me first," or "When you left me waiting at the restaurant for an hour." I'm even amazed at how many people can twist an *I-statement* into a *You-statement* and are puzzled at why their *healthy* communication isn't working. For example, I have heard individuals share, "When the bills were overdue, and I started getting phone calls from creditors wondering why you haven't been paying anything that you were supposed to be paying, and now you are about to ruin our credit…" What starts out as an *I-statement* quickly morphs into a *You-statement* that will yield a defensive response.

The second part of our *I-statement* template says, "I felt _____." Please note that we are sharing emotions, not thoughts. If we refer to our emotions list, we might share, "I felt angry, disrespected, scared, and a little sad." Perhaps we only felt one thing. If so, then we only share the one emotion. If we felt multiple emotions, sharing all of the emotions associated with the incident we just described is important.

The last part of the format is the one usually left out or ignored. Perhaps the hardest part is where I end with the statement, "I just wanted to share that with you." When we share with someone, we usually want action, we want some resolution that makes us feel better. However, healthy communication is not about sharing in order to get a desired response. Healthy communication is about sharing what I am thinking and feeling in a healthy, respectful way simply because that is a requirement for me to be healthy. I must share to keep resentments from piling up inside of me and weighing me down emotionally.

If I am only willing to share my thoughts and feelings given the guarantee of a certain response or outcome, I am not communicating in a healthy manner. Whether conscious or unconscious, I am manipulating the situation. I am, in essence, saying that I am not willing to be healthy unless I get what I want from someone else. The other person will never feel good from this type of exchange, and the conversation (manipulation) will never ultimately yield the abundant, peace-filled relationship I desire.

Ending my communication with, "I just wanted to share that with you," frees both my partner and myself from needing or requiring a resolution and allows space for both of us to process what I have just shared. However they choose to respond, my communication is healthy if I have been able to share my thoughts and feelings in a way that is calm and respectful.

Learning to Listen

Listening is the next component of healthy communication and is our greatest tool if we are willing to learn and practice. Many people will describe themselves as great listeners, but the only person they truly like to hear is themselves. They interrupt, they dismiss, they can never hear someone else's experience because the only valid experience in their mind is theirs. Sadly, that is not health.

Actively, attentively listening requires me to feel safe enough with myself so I can truly lean in and hear my partner or friend speaking. As the listener, I am to lay aside any agenda I have so I might simply *be* with another. I need to try to understand their experience as different, as real, and as unique as my own experience. Active listening allows space for two experiences to be shared, heard, and potentially understood. Listening nurtures connection and builds intimacy.

I cannot truly listen or sit with my friend if I have a weapon in my hand. My awareness would be on my weapon as a means to keep me safe. My weapons or defenses therefore keep me from the kind of intimacy and connection I desire. When I no longer need weapons or defenses to keep me safe, I am able to open myself to others in a way that is freeing.

When I am teaching clients how to build their active listening skills, I will encourage them to give their partner the floor in a discussion, to allow them to speak whatever they need or want to share, as long as they are calm and respectful. Once their partner is done, I encourage them to summarize what they thought they heard their partner share first before they respond or take the floor to share. If their partner affirms they heard the message correctly, they can then move on to share themselves, but if they didn't get the message right, they continue to listen and then summarize until their partner affirms that they got what the partner said/ meant. Then and only then can the listener assume the floor and begin to share, again, as long as they, too, are healthy and respectful.

Active listening teaches us how to listen to someone else while they are speaking instead of planning our rebuttal or defense for when they are finished. They are allowed to be heard, to finish their thoughts in a way that is meaningful to them. If we truly want to be heard, logically others would like the same opportunity. Often, once we can hear our partner's perspective, we see whatever our grievance might be in a new light, and perhaps that new understanding can help keep us on the same team instead of pitting us against each other.

The Qualities That Destroy Communication

In looking at what healthy communication is, we must also address what healthy communication isn't. Healthy communication has no need to defend. Even if my friend is not offering openness, kindness, or respect to me, I always have a choice as to how I respond. I can make the choice to calmly, respectfully hold onto myself and my experience. I can also make the choice to use negative defenses as weapons to keep me safe.

John Gottman, psychologist and founder of the Love Lab at the University of Washington, and later the Gottman Institute, coined the term *Four Horseman of the Apocalypse* to define the four defenses he has researched and found to be most destructive to relationships – criticism, contempt, defensiveness, and stonewalling.[44]

A complaint describes a specific issue, whereas a criticism is more a universal judgment or attack on our partner's character. Criticisms become very black or white generalizations that often contain the words *always* and *never*. An example might be, "You always take your mother's side of everything," or "You're never here for me or the kids." Criticisms make the environment safe for us at our partner's expense.

Contempt takes criticism one step further and attacks our partner's sense of self with the intent to harm or abuse them. Contempt may come in the form of name-calling or belittling, or may be noticed in sarcasm or mocking humor. We may also show contempt in our body language with sneering or eye-rolling. Any of these behaviors, as innocent or funny as they may seem, will absolutely destroy our relationships.

Early in my marriage, I realized the sarcasm I thought was humorous wasn't so humorous to my husband. Sarcasm is a cutting or ironic remark used to make the victim the butt of the joke. Sarcasm is always humor at someone else's expense. We see sarcasm rampant on sitcoms, reality TV, and late night comedy. We applaud sarcasm as wit, and well-placed zingers with praise

---

44 John Gottman, *Seven Principles For Making Marriage Work* (New York: Three Rivers Press, 1999), 27.

and laughter. However, sarcasm is always hurtful to someone and is deadly to any EA or peace in a relationship.

Once I became aware of my sarcasm and the effects on my relationship, I worked hard to replace those barbs with kindness and respect. I learned how to share my thoughts and feelings clearly and directly instead of using sarcasm as a means of indirect communication. The relationship became safer and healthier, and I learned to find my humor elsewhere.

Defensiveness is the act of making ourselves the victim in order to keep us safe from a perceived attack. Most parents with teenagers have come face to face with defensiveness at some point during their children's adolescence. We have gone to our children with a complaint about their room, their homework, or their behavior, and their immediate response has been: 1) every excuse under the sun why it isn't their fault; 2) countering our complaint with a complaint of their own as to why it can't get done; 3) "Yes, but..."– starting off agreeing but then quickly disagreeing about why it can't or shouldn't be done; 4) whining with the "it's not fair" or "nobody understands" card. Somewhere in the mix there is usually some reason we were to blame.

However, many of us adults use the same defensive tactics in our adult relationships we used as teenagers. The results will always be the same–frustration and resentment. The relationship is always the loser.

The last of the *Four Horseman of the Apocalypse* is stonewalling. Stonewalling is different from taking a time-out. Taking a time-out is always for the purpose of calming ourselves so we can re-engage our partner and continue the discussion productively. Stonewalling, on the other hand, is a defense mechanism that disengages or withdraws from our partner to avoid conflict.

Sometimes stonewallers will give the silent treatment for hours, even days, or weeks. Sometimes they will give monosyllabic responses. Other times they distance or remove themselves physically from any environment where there could be an argument. The implication is this: *if there is any chance of conflict, I will cut you off, I will separate myself from you until I feel certain there will be no more conflict and, quite possibly, punish you enough so you think twice next time before you contemplate confronting me again.*

Whether our weapon of choice is stonewalling, defensiveness, contempt, or criticism, we all have tendencies toward certain defense mechanisms we learned early on to keep us safe or perhaps even to survive. Those defense mechanisms will destroy the fabric and beauty of any relationship. They will undermine the safety, respect, and trust that every relationship needs to thrive.

The Power of One

Once we become aware of our defenses, we are empowered to begin building new ways to engage in our relationships. We can keep ourselves safe no matter what. We can open ourselves to hear another's experience, and we can open ourselves to sharing our experience. We can communicate calmly, clearly, and directly. We can lay aside our need to defend, our need to win at all costs, and even our need to change our partner. As we do, we will learn we can come into safe contact with others and enjoy the process of building relationship.

We are the key. We own responsibility for ourselves in our communication, our life, and our relationships. We cannot ask or require another person to take responsibility for our safety, happiness, or well-being. This is the essence of our work with

God and ourselves. Our relationships are merely the canvas on which we get to practice and experiment.

We can never blame another for our *lack of,* whether a lack of safety, a lack of peace, or a lack of having our needs met. The responsibility for us ultimately lies with us. We are in charge of our safety, peace, even our needs. If something must come from another, we are in charge of using our voice to speak our thoughts, feelings, and needs in a healthy, respectful way.

We do not even need our partners or friends to be healthy in order for us to be healthy. Many people give up and say that they cannot use healthy communication if their partner doesn't use healthy communication; that they cannot change unless their partner is willing to change.

If our health or emotional well-being is dependent upon what another person does or does not do, on what they promise to do or not to do, our emotional health is on shaky ground. The more I am able to shift my focus from someone else as the key to my peace, to me as the key to my peace, the more likely I am to find peace. The person over whom I have the greatest amount of control and influence is me. Therefore, even if my partner is not choosing EA, I can choose EA; I can experience the benefits of EA even if my partner doesn't. Better still, I can do this, even if my partner doesn't make my growth on this journey easier for me.

Choosing EA does not mean that we stay in abusive relationships. Our next step in pursuing health will be to recognize and understand healthy boundaries. If an environment is not physically or emotionally safe for us, we must create healthy boundaries that will keep us safe.

Healthy communication is simply the first step in taking all of the health and peace that we have been cultivating internally and beginning to share our new-found self in our relationships. When we share, we may be frightened at first, but we will feel good.

We feel good because we don't have to carry around excess emotional baggage and can unpack our emotions with others, healthfully and effectively, right at the moment. The negativity and drama in our relationships are reduced. Then we get to enjoy the people in our lives and perhaps connect with them in a deeper way than we ever thought possible.

....

Stepping Stones

- How emotionally honest are you in your relationships? Do you *ping* well with others, or is that something difficult for you to do?

- When you are with others, focus on remaining connected with yourself. Notice your thoughts, feelings, and anxiety level; also notice any physical sensations in your body. Journal later about the things you noticed.

- As you journal, begin to write down how you would like to respond. Practice using *I-statements* as well as the format, "When _____ happened, I felt _____, and I just wanted to share that with you." ***Be careful that your *I-statements* don't morph into *You-statements*.

- Practice your active listening skills with others. As you sit with them, notice your breathing as well as your heart rate. Begin to calm yourself and slow your breathing. Allow yourself to be in the moment and simply listen. Focus on trying to understand or learn something new about the other person. When they finish, summarize what you think you heard them say and ask if you heard them correctly. Keep repeating this until you are correct. Then, if you would like to share, share your thoughts and feelings in a healthy, respectful way.

- Which of Gottman's *Four Horseman of the Apocalypse* do you tend to use in your relationships? As you list them, begin to practice calming yourself in those moments, and write down alternative ways to directly communicate your thoughts and feelings without using criticism, contempt, defensiveness, or stonewalling.

- Do you tend to blame others for the problems in your relationships? Write down the problems for which you are responsible and the things you need to change to resolve the problems and improve the relationship.

- How emotionally safe do you feel in your relationships? What do you need to do in order to feel safer? Who makes you safe? Could you be in charge of your safety? Can you trust that you are safe enough with God? Can you learn how to keep yourself safe, to know when you are not safe, and to know the appropriate ways to keep yourself safe?

Chapter Fifteen

FREEING OTHERS AS I FREE MYSELF

*When we accept others' freedom, we don't get angry, feel guilty, or
withdraw our love when they set boundaries with us. When we
accept other's freedom, we feel better about our own.*[45]

—Dr. Henry Cloud, and Dr. John Townsend

No One Likes To Be Controlled

Have you ever had the experience of trying to get your child to
eat something they did not want to eat? Have you ever tried to
get your spouse to mow the lawn, balance the checkbook, cook
dinner, or even go to church when they didn't want to?

We'd like to think we know what is best for those around us.
However, most of the time compelling someone to do something
against their will doesn't go so well. Even if we can get them to
do what we want, they are not happy, and they usually end up

---

45 Henry Cloud and John Townsend, *Boundaries* (Grand Rapids, MI: Zondervan, 1992), 90.

feeling resentful and distant towards us in the end.

None of us like to be told what to do. We don't like to feel controlled, coerced, or manipulated into doing things. We don't like to feel pressure to *do* from our spouses. We don't like to feel pressure to *do* from our friends. We certainly don't like to feel pressure to *do* from our bosses, our government, perhaps even God. We all like the freedom to choose.

So when we focus our energy in relationships on getting someone to do something we want or may even legitimately need, we set ourselves up for frustration, hurt, and anger. We feel rejected and unloved. What if our loved one is unable or unwilling to meet our request? Our emotional health is left hanging by a thread when we are dependent upon someone else. There is no Emotional Abundance in that. As we defined earlier, Emotional Abundance, or EA, is the over-sufficient supply, the overflowing fullness that happens in our lives and relationships as we learn to manage our emotions effectively so we can appropriately respond to the people and circumstances around us.

Good Fences Do Make Good Neighbors

Many times when I attempt to describe relationship to clients, I ask them to imagine living in a neighborhood where their individual property backs up to the property of their loved one. Between their backyards is a common area with some grass, trees, and perhaps even a picnic table. The common area is where their relationship exists. Both are responsible to maintain their individual backyards, and they share in the maintenance of the common area. Each does the chores for the common area that are the most meaningful to them. Ideally, they work together and enjoy their shared space.

If one partner chooses not to help maintain the common area, the other is free to maintain that portion or not, whatever is meaningful to them. However, if they feel coerced to do their partner's chores, they will soon end up feeling resentful toward them and, even though the common area is well-maintained, neither will enjoy that place or each other.

If they choose not to do their partner's chores for them, there are also consequences. The common area will become overgrown and unkempt. The garden and the benches will deteriorate. Some areas will no longer be beautiful for them to enjoy. There will be less clear space for them to sit together and enjoy each other. In order for the common area to flourish, there must be safety, mutuality, openness, respect, and compassion. If these qualities are not at work, the area can survive, but thriving will be difficult. Each individual is empowered only to control and make choices about those things that are in their control. One person can never control their loved one's choice to invest in their common area and vice versa.

There is a fence surrounding the common area with two gates on each side, one leading in from one partner's backyard, the other leading in from the other's backyard. While they can enjoy the shared space and even walk near the fence, neither is free to enter the other's backyard.

Taking Care of My Backyard

Our backyard is ours alone. We have responsibilities no one else can do for us. We plant, we mow, we weed. God waters, God nurtures with sun, God grows. The common area is simply the area where we get to experience, celebrate, and cheer each other along on our journeys. Sometimes the common area is the place where we cry with and pray for each other in our pain.

There are times, emotionally speaking, when we ask others to come into our backyard, and do something for us they cannot or perhaps should not do. There are times when others ask, even beg us to come into their backyard and do something for them we cannot or should not do.

Our backyards represent our emotional selves and the fences are our boundaries. Boundaries are the parameters or limits we establish in our relationships that allow us to know where we end and where another begins. Healthy boundaries allow us to breathe *LIFE* into our relationships, and we use them to *FREE* others as we free ourselves.

Many people think of boundaries as confining, controlling, punitive, or hurtful, not freeing—but they are. They are freeing because they allow us to express and embrace our individuality. They are freeing because they allow us to own responsibility for our individual thoughts, feelings, and choices. Boundaries free us from the pressure and pain of unrealistic expectations. They are one of the greatest gifts to any relationship.

Boundaries Free Us To Express Our Individuality

Boundaries allow us embrace our individuality, to have our identity, beliefs and values, passions and purpose. For spouses, friends, and others with whom we are in relationship, respect is allowing them their boundaries as well. We cannot build EA in our relationships by believing everyone should be, think, or feel exactly the way we do. God created all of us thoughtfully and uniquely. We are all on our individual journeys with God and are growing both in different ways and at different paces.

If we are parents with children, we need to understand we cannot force our sons and daughters to be just like us, we cannot compel them as they grow to live exactly as we do, or have the same beliefs and values we do. That does not mean, when we see our children doing destructive things and making poor choices, we sit by and say nothing. The meaning is we continue to love our children passionately as we share with them our concerns, our thoughts and feelings, as well as our beliefs and values. If they are minors, there should certainly be consequences for poor choices. But if they are adults and not dependent on us financially or emotionally, we are empowered only with prayer, to love, and to share, as long as our sharing is both calm and respectful.

The more we can free our loved ones to pursue their growth, to discover more of their identity, to acknowledge their beliefs and values, and even acquire new passions along the way, the more we will be able to accept them and love them as they are, right where they are. We are also asked to free them even when they should choose *not* to pursue their growth.

In freeing others, we will be able to take all of the energies we have focused on needing those around us to change (which we cannot control) and use those energies to change ourselves. We are empowered to bring change into our lives, and every choice we make to free others removes pressure from the relationship that the relationship was never meant to carry.

There are no two of us alike. In His infinite wisdom and love, God draws us to a person who is uniquely different from us. Their differences create opportunities for our growth. God can use those differences as tools for our healing on our journey if we are willing to let Him.

EA doesn't mean that I surround myself only with people who are exactly like me. EA means, because I am anchored solidly in God and have taken the time to discover and strengthen my core identity, I can sit equally with those who are like-minded as well as with those who are not, without fear that I will change and without demanding those around me to change.

Boundaries Free Us to Own Our Thoughts, Feelings, and Choices

I am responsible for my thoughts, feelings, and choices – to manage them, calm them, and make decisions about them for myself. No one else can do that for me. Likewise, my friends and loved ones are responsible for their thoughts, feelings, and choices, to manage them, to calm them, and to make decisions for themselves based on them.

If I am unhappy, exhausted, or anxious, I am responsible for those feelings. I am also responsible for understanding what those feelings are about, where they are coming from, and what I need to do in order to change them. That may mean I need to draw a boundary and say no to some activities to get better rest. I may need to rebalance my schedule in order to prioritize my spouse or family. I may need to begin speaking what I am thinking and feeling to those around me in a healthy, respectful way so I don't build up resentments that leave me feeling angry and bitter.

Again, speaking what I am thinking and feeling should never be for the purpose of getting a desired response or resolution. I share my thoughts and feelings because I am more healthy, more emotionally-abundant when I do so. Once I've shared, I then free my loved one to have whatever reaction or response they need.

Sharing should never be conditional; if sharing is, the relationship cannot be healthy, authentic, or free.

I am strengthened by recognizing that someone else doesn't hold the keys to my peace. I hold the keys to my peace alone with God. As I free myself to unlock the doors of my internal self and allow God to be the source of my healing, I will find healing. Somewhere in the process I will also find I don't need so much from my spouse, my children, or my friends. Because I need less from them, I can simply enjoy them and free them to make choices for themselves on their journeys.

Boundaries Allow Us To Own the Consequences of Our Choices

As a natural consequence of loving our children, we want to remove anything from their lives that would be painful. Sometimes we rescue our children; sometimes we rescue our spouses, parents, siblings, co-workers, or friends. If we're being totally honest, sometimes we even expect them to step in and rescue us from the consequences of our unhealthy choices. However, if we desire peace in our relationships, rescuing is seldom the healthiest option.

Every time we rescue, we are removing an opportunity for someone to learn and grow. Every time we rescue, we remove God from His position in our loved one's life and place ourselves in His position as God in their life. Children don't learn from a lecture, spouses don't change from nagging, and friends can't grow from coddling. We all learn from owning responsibility for our choices and learning from the consequences that come with those choices, whether they are positive or negative. By freeing ourselves and others to own responsibility for our thoughts, feelings, and choices, we free our relationships to become gardens of abundance, and that brings peace.

Boundaries Free Us from the Pressure and Pain of Unrealistic Expectations

Whether our expectations are derived from the movies we watch, the music we listen to, or the relationships around us, most of us seem to come to our relationships with many expectations of what that relationship will mean to us, what that relationship will *do* for us. Perhaps, we think, a relationship will save us from our dysfunctional family of origin. Maybe another person will fill us, fix us, provide for us, and give us everything we desire. When they don't, we are left hopeless, broken, angry, and disappointed.

Many of us live with the pressure of needing or trying to be the *perfect* wife, the *perfect* mother, the *perfect* employee, or the *perfect* friend because we feel that is what is expected of us in relationship. The truth is no one can live up to the pressure of trying to be perfect. We were not meant to be everything to our loved ones, and they were not meant to be everything to us.

Boundaries create safety because they allow us to know what is healthy to expect and what is not. They nurture an environment where there is clarity surrounding each partner's responsibilities. Boundaries allow movement and freedom for individuals to continue to grow and flourish within the context of the relationship, rather than outgrowing the relationship.

Speaking and Enforcing Our Boundaries

As a pre-requisite for drawing healthy boundaries, we must first have done the work of identity investing discussed in Section Two. A solid sense of self is necessary so we can define what our boundaries are and know where to place them. We must also have learned from Section Two how to listen to and trust our inner voice. When we realize a boundary has been crossed, we can speak our thoughts and feelings in order to construct or reinforce healthy boundaries.

Are there times when someone asks something of you, and you get an immediate knot in your stomach? That's usually your inner voice telling you something's not right, that a boundary of respect or responsibility has been violated. As we learn to listen to our inner voice, we can begin to process what boundary has been crossed. We can define for ourselves the things we could feel good doing as well as the things we do not feel good doing for someone else.

Once we've spoken a boundary clearly and respectfully, we must enforce the line. Many of us get tripped up at this point in the process. How many times have we as parents spoken a boundary to our children and ultimately found ourselves giving in to their requests or demands? We give them the keys to the car though they have been consistently disrespectful and haven't cleaned their room in months. We always have a good reason (or excuse) we use to rationalize our decision, but the truth is, we violated our own boundary. At the same time, we are teaching our children that our boundaries are not actual boundaries and that when we say, "No," we don't mean "no."

Sometimes we have given our loved ones money for the ump-teenth time, even though we know they have been irresponsible with their money and have yet to pay us back even one dime they owe us from all of the times before. We keep lending them money over and over again. We feel our frustration mounting, but for some reason we find we simply cannot say the magic word, "no."

Many of us feel guilty drawing a boundary. We feel we are being mean and hurtful to our loved ones. We feel that as Christians, we are supposed to be everything to everyone, all of the time. However, on the contrary, drawing a boundary for ourselves frees our loved ones to find the solutions to their problems within themselves and with God. Allowing them to do so develops their belief they are powerful and competent enough to meet their own needs and strengthens their faith in the process.

If we have spent most of our lives with few boundaries or unhealthy ones, others may take some time to understand and respect them. They might not like our boundaries at first. They might respond negatively to our boundaries. They might do anything they can—act pitiful, angry, even hostile towards our boundaries—to undermine them. Our boundaries aren't wrong or unhealthy—more likely our loved ones have gotten used to us doing something for them they should be doing for themselves and they want our help to continue.

Going to the trouble of drawing boundaries and even speaking them requires us to follow through with them if we are going to build EA into our relationships. Even if others don't like our boundaries, we must be committed to them and consistent with them. When we falter, we should offer compassion to ourselves, and then get back up and try again.

Our rule of thumb thus far—we keep ourselves calm, centered, and connected, we speak what we are thinking and feeling in a healthy, respectful way to those around us, we free others to react or respond in whatever way they choose, and then we draw the physical or emotional boundaries that are needed to keep us safe.

Boundaries Are Not Cut-Offs

Many people feel when there is a disagreement or dissatisfaction in a relationship, cutting the relationship off is a way of drawing a healthy boundary. Unfortunately, that is not necessarily true. Boundaries allow us to keep ourselves safe in the context of a relationship while working through difficulties along the way. Cut-offs unconsciously convey that unless the other person does the work for us to feel safe, we cannot remain in the relationship. If they hold us accountable, share any concerns, disagree in any way, we will cut off the relationship. While there are times when the only resolution in a toxic relationship is a cut-off, dissolution should be an option of last resort.

Healthy boundaries don't keep us isolated from those we love, but they actually allow us to experience greater intimacy and inter-dependence because they preserve the integrity of the individuals and allow two selves to safely and freely come together in order to experience each other. That, for me, is the truest meaning of relationship.

Stepping Stones

- As you reflect on your life today, what relationships share the most common area in your emotional backyard? Write down the qualities that make the shared space of each relationship the most meaningful and enjoyable for you. (i.e., common interests, shared values, humor, etc.)

- Are there areas where you have asked others to do things for you emotionally that are not theirs to do? Are there areas where others have asked you to do things for them emotionally that are not yours to do?

- List areas in each relationship where you might need to draw one or more boundaries. What lets you know that a boundary might be needed? What should that boundary look like? What could you feel good doing for your loved one; what would you *not* feel good doing for them?

- Begin to pray over these boundaries. Practice speaking them. Rehearse what implementing them looks like. Look for opportunities to speak them to those around you.

- What kind of response do you anticipate from drawing a specific boundary? Can you free that person to have whatever response they need to have, knowing that you can draw boundaries to keep yourself physically and emotionally safe?

- Do you have difficulty accepting them when others draw boundaries for themselves in your relationship? Journal how you feel when this happens.

- Are there things you have asked others to do for you that perhaps you could do for yourself? List some of the things that come to mind.

- Is this want or need legitimate? Can you meet the want or need without someone else? How could you begin to meet that want or need yourself with God's help?

- If your need cannot be met without someone else's participation, begin to accept the absence of the unmet want or need and grieve the loss, whether the loss is temporary or permanent.

- Write a list of things you could change about your life today that would make your life feel more satisfying or meaningful and don't require you to abandon your commitments.

Chapter Sixteen

Engaging Collaborative Conflict-Resolution

You can't shake hands with a clenched fist.[46]
—Indira Gandhi

Understanding the Nature of Conflict

The word *conflict* basically means a struggle or clash of incompatible forces. Conflict is something rarely desired, yet something all of us have experienced on one occasion or another. Some people tend to avoid conflict at all cost. Others seem drawn to the battle like a moth to a flame.

The truth is conflict can be a normal, even healthy part of human relationships. Conflict itself is not bad. How we handle conflict is what ultimately determines the outcome. When handled poorly, conflict can be destructive to a relationship and the

---

46 Indira Gandhi. BrainyQuote.com, Xplore Inc., 2014. http://www.brainyquote.com/quotes/quotes/i/indiragand100042.html, accessed June 6, 2014.

individuals involved, but when handled well, conflict can grow and strengthen Emotional Abundance (EA) in a relationship. EA allows us to respond appropriately to the people and circumstances around us as we increase our ability to feel, process, and manage our emotions.

Conflict is more than just a difference of opinion or disagreement. I can disagree with someone on a variety of issues—economics, politics, faith, education, and so on. I can have a different perspective, even different beliefs and values. However, when I become emotionally engaged to the point the disagreement becomes a source of criticism or judgment, when the difference of opinion remains unresolved for a length of time, or when either of our emotional needs are never heard, respected, or addressed, that's when a disagreement turns into a conflict.

Recognizing Our Conflict Style

We all have instinctual reactions and responses to conflict. Most of what we have learned to believe about conflict and how we have learned to respond is based on our early childhood experiences within our families of origin. These experiences become the framework for how we experience and deal with conflict in our adult relationships.

Researchers Kenneth Thomas and Ralph Kilmann have identified five main styles of dealing with conflict: avoidant, accommodating, competing, compromising, and collaborative.[47] While no individual employs a single style, we typically have preferred conflict resolution styles we use more than others, perhaps

---

47 Kenneth Thomas, *Thomas-Kilmann Conflict Mode Instrument* (Mountain View, CA: CPP, Inc., 2002).

because of personality and/or experience. We all have the ability, however, to grow beyond our preferred styles and incorporate healthier approaches to dealing with conflict.

Each style is composed of some measure of cooperativeness and assertiveness. Cooperativeness is the quality focused on meeting the other person's needs; assertiveness is the quality focused on meeting our individual needs. Health lies not in one extreme or the other. In finding the right balance of cooperativeness and assertiveness where I can respect and value my thoughts, feelings, and needs while at the same time respecting and valuing another person's thoughts, feelings, and needs, I can create an environment where both perspectives can be considered and mutual solutions can be negotiated.

Many individuals experience conflict as something terrible to be strictly avoided for fear of what the outcome might be. This describes the *avoidant* style of conflict. Avoiders try to create a pretend world where everything appears perfect. If they don't look at conflict, they believe conflict doesn't exist. In brushing conflict under the rug, they feel all of its inherent messiness will disappear and everything will become perfect again. Some avoiders might withdraw or shut-down while others prefer to stonewall, using tactics to delay or sidestep a discussion.

Somehow avoiders instinctively know everything is not perfect. Whether conscious or unconscious, the tension can be felt bubbling just beneath the surface. This style demonstrates low levels of cooperativeness and assertiveness. Avoiders are not motivated to act out of concern for others or concern for themselves. They would simply rather not deal with the conflict at all. However, there usually comes a time when there isn't a rug big enough to hide all of the hurts and resentments that have built up and something tragic has to occur in order to learn different ways of dealing with conflict.

Have you ever encountered someone who always seems to give in when faced with conflict? They never seem able to stake out a position or hold onto their thoughts, feelings, or needs if those emotions conflict with someone else's. These individuals have an *accommodating* style of conflict. Accommodators have high levels of cooperativeness and low levels of assertiveness. Some might call these individuals *peacemakers*, especially in the church, but what little peace is gained in the short-term is usually overshadowed by longer-term resentment. Successful conflict-resolution only occurs when both parties' thoughts, feelings, and needs can be heard and negotiated to a mutually satisfactory conclusion.

Whenever I choose *not* to speak my thoughts and feelings in a healthy, respectful way, I abandon a piece of myself. The emotional consequence of this will always be the same. I will feel a tiny bit of resentment inside for not having had the opportunity or courage to be heard. As a recovering avoider/accommodator, I have learned both approaches want to remove the conflict as quickly as possible with the belief that all conflict is negative. The avoider in me simply wants to run away from the situation, while the accommodator in me wants to give in so I don't displease anyone, and the relationship can get back to normal.

Some individuals experience conflict in an angry, explosive way. The rules of their game are simple – kill or be killed, figuratively speaking. This is a *competing* conflict style. As the name implies, there is a low level of cooperativeness and a high level of assertiveness with this approach. Thoughts and feelings cannot be spoken, they must be screamed. Anytime there is a disagreement or difference of perspective, values, or needs, the battle drums start practicing for the imminent siege. Power for these individuals is not something to be shared, but is something to be fought for and claimed for themselves, usually at someone else's expense.

Because they don't run from conflict, many feel they are dealing with such disagreements in a healthier way by getting out all of the intense emotions. Unfortunately, anger and aggression are not synonymous with respect and resolution. The emotions and words exchanged in the heat of battle are destructive. Long after the flames of conflict have dissipated; the wounds from words spoken in anger still smolder deep inside.

As we move toward healthier approaches to conflict-resolution, we discover individuals who don't shy away from conflict, who can have moderate levels of cooperativeness and assertiveness. These individuals can focus on minimizing the negative. They seem adept at understanding the art of negotiation. These individuals practice a *compromising* conflict style.

They can hear and be heard. They believe if each individual gives a little here and there, each can win some things and let go of other things. This style is a blend of give-and-take that, they believe, brings about the ultimate resolution.

Perhaps the healthiest approach to conflict resolution is the *collaborative* style. This approach goes one step further than the compromising style. Collaborators share higher levels of both cooperativeness and assertiveness. They move beyond minimizing the negative to creating the positive that will be a win-win for everyone involved. They can truly listen to the other individual's thoughts, feelings, and needs as well as to respectfully share their own.

This approach shifts from seeing two parties at odds, to seeing two parties on the same team working toward a mutual goal.

Their focus is on how to overcome obstacles in order to build a maximizing solution creatively.

Recognizing our preferred conflict style(s) is an important step in being able to identify where we are. Sometimes seeing where we are can also allow us to see how we arrived here. Yet, for most of us, our current emotional location is not our ultimate destination if peace in our relationships is our desire. We can learn how to walk through conflict well and strategize to resolve whatever differences we have. The choice is ours.

Engaging Collaborative Conflict Resolution

This step will be next to impossible if we have not done our work in the preceding sections. If we cannot yet *Live* calmly, connected, and centered, we will not be able to create a calm environment, especially when stress and emotions are running high. Attempting to create a compassionate, cooperative environment will prove futile if we continue to see our loved ones as adversaries to win a battle against instead of friends with whom we desire to build a bridge.

We will be ready to enter into conflict resolution only after we can arrive at a place of calm, when we've done our individual work to *Invest* in healthy communication in order to identify, understand, and articulate our thoughts and feelings to one another. For some, the anxiety associated with conflict creates such a confused and disorganized mind that we might need some time to calm ourselves thoroughly and be able to process exactly what we are thinking and feeling. Whether the calming takes a few minutes or a few days, this step is important and should not be ignored.

Fostering a Compassionate Environment

Compassion is probably not at the forefront of our minds when we are thinking about being in conflict with a loved one. We are usually adept at seeing our side in an argument, but few of us can genuinely lay aside our *rightness* in order to show compassion towards a friend with whom we are conflicted.

Compassion is more than just seeing or showing empathy for another person's perspective. Compassion desires to offer understanding and favor in the face of potential uncertainty. Compassion is a quality that allows us to **Free** others as we free ourselves. Compassion brings openness and objectivity to the discussion table instead of defensiveness and judgment. True compassion is the breeding ground for healing and growth in relationships.

Compassion builds a foundation for cooperation to flourish. A vital function of **Engaging** Collaborative Conflict Resolution cooperation requires two individuals to work together towards a shared goal. If we have two different goals and we are unwilling to join forces in defining a mutual outcome, we will be less likely to resolve conflict successfully. Though we cannot control another's level of calm, compassion, or cooperation, we can strengthen the skill for ourselves. That alone will have a positive impact on how we feel about conflict, and how we work through conflict, both now and in the future.

Sharing Our Thoughts and Feelings About the Problem

How we share depends upon the dynamic of the conflict. If I have identified I am the individual who is having the problem in the relationship, then sharing my thoughts and feelings first is important. Sometimes, when we have set up a time to talk, the other person may or may not have any notion of a problem.

What is vital, as always, is whatever we share needs to be both healthy and respectful. When we can identify a specific complaint and describe our feelings about that complaint, we reduce the likelihood of defensive responses. Being intentional to eliminate any criticism, contempt, defensiveness, or stonewalling maintains the safety and openness for both individuals to continue the discussion. Once someone's defenses are raised, hope for productive conversation dims.

If both individuals came to the discussion already aware of and engaged with the problem, who shares first is not crucial. However, by allowing the other to share first, we are creating the environment of compassion and cooperation we desire. We are saying, in an indirect way, "I want to hear from you. I want to understand you better so I can factor your thoughts, feelings, and needs into the equation."

Just as some individuals are great at creating boundaries for themselves while they have trouble respecting anyone else's, some individuals are great at sharing their thoughts and feelings while they are not so great at listening to someone else's. We must move beyond experiencing everything from our perspective to being able to see ourselves as a part of someone else's experience. We simply cannot do this if we are unwilling or unable to truly lean in and listen to them.

If the other individual shares first, before we do anything else, our job is to reflect back to them what we thought we heard them say. Whether we agree or not, the point is we are working to understand their perspective better. Our job is not to tell anyone they shouldn't feel what they are feeling, that their feelings are bad or wrong, or to correct their feelings. Our job, if we want to learn collaborative conflict resolution, is to offer a safe place for others to share their feelings and to reflect our understanding of them back as a sign of respect.

No matter whether someone else has learned collaborative conflict resolution skills or not, no matter if they use healthy communication skills or not, we are forever empowered to choose health for ourselves. Even in this setting, if our loved one is sharing and they become critical and defensive towards us, this does not mean that we simply give up and join in with them. We must keep our focus on remaining calm, compassionate, and coopera-tive, as much as possible, whether anyone else joins us or not. *If it is possible, as far as it depends on you, live at peace with everyone.* (Romans 12:18 NIV)

Looking For Common Ground

Once each has shared, the next step is to see if there are areas on which we can agree. Perhaps we can agree on a desired outcome, perhaps we can agree on a shared feeling or perspective. This is a beginning.

At this point, many individuals tend to rush towards a resolution. Don't. Enjoy the moments of finding common ground. They are precious gems that will potentially become stepping-stones toward the ultimate outcome.

As we continue to explore common ground, we can begin to see if there are places where we could share power. Is this a situation where I need to hold onto all of the power? Is my holding none of the power acceptable? Perhaps there could be a way that both of us could share the power and feel satisfied. If so, what might that look like? How could that feel different from what each of us is feeling right now?

This is where we either settle for compromise or we push together collaboratively. Is there a possibility we could be on the same team? What is the force out there we could be fighting against together? Strategizing for ways both of us can win creates a resolution both individuals can get excited about and be motivated to pursue. At times, compromise is the best outcome possible. If there is the potential for something better, we can do our part to bring about the successful resolution.

Collaboration Requires Openness To Accountability

We have the tendency to see our side and only our side; our loved one sees their side. Because we are human, in truth we are capable of hurting others, even if the hurt is unintentional. If we are to become collaborators when working through conflict, if we want others to be open to accountability when they have hurt us, we must be open to accountability as well. We must have the courage to look in the mirror and see how our words or behaviors have negatively impacted someone else.

In recognizing we have hurt another, the first step is to own responsibility for our words or actions. Sometimes our reaction is to excuse, explain, rationalize, or minimize our behavior. Sometimes we get defensive. We play the victim, perhaps at times the martyr. We are not owning responsibility. I can only own the situation if I can look at myself and my behaviors directly and accept the full weight of responsibility for how my words or actions have wounded another. Acceptance allows me to carry the burden of hurt, not for the purpose of producing shame, guilt, or feelings of worthlessness, but for the purpose of producing healing.

Once I own responsibility, I can repent, which is to express sincere remorse or regret. I can ask for forgiveness, and I can determine what amends should be made. If I was critical or condemning of a friend, my amends might be in working to become more compassionate and loving instead. If I was controlling or manipulative, my amends might be in learning how to reel in my selfish impulses while learning to free others to do the same for themselves. If I had a habit of lying or even telling half-truths, perhaps my amends could be in working to become open, honest, and transparent so I could rebuild the trust in the relationship.

This process is quite different from simply apologizing. Most of us have been in a relationship where someone apologizes repetitively. Many of these apologies come from *avoiders* or *accommodators* who don't want to deal with an issue, but simply want to move quickly past the unpleasantness. Accommodating isn't owning responsibility in the same way that apologizing isn't repenting. The reason is individuals who apologize never own the full weight of responsibility for their words or behaviors. Because of this, they cannot sincerely repent and ask forgiveness, nor are they inclined to make amends. They simply want to apologize and move on, without ever experiencing true healing.

Conflicts That Cannot Be Resolved

There may be times in working through conflict, when a loved one shares a problem with us. They offer their thoughts and feelings. We want to be compassionate, we do our best to be open to accountability, yet as we evaluate the situation, we realize we simply do not have ownership of the problem, or even part of the problem. Owning responsibility for a problem, just for the sake of peace, is never a healthy option. If we cannot own responsibility, we can still respectfully listen, we can offer compassion, and we can do our best to express our desire to move forward together. Just because someone is having a problem doesn't automatically mean the problem is ours.

There might be a situation where we have a legitimate problem with someone. We have shared how their words or behaviors have been tremendously hurtful to us and yet they refuse to own responsibility. How we should act or respond then is difficult to know. If we have respectfully shared our thoughts and feelings and our loved one doesn't hear, understand, or respect what we have to say, we must free them to respond in whatever way they choose. We cannot force someone to be open to accountability, and we certainly can never push anyone who refuses to own responsibility.

Choosing Forgiveness

Of primary importance here is what *we* do. *We* have the power to choose forgiveness despite the circumstances. Forgiveness is by no means a magic bullet that means somehow everything is okay. What choosing forgiveness means is I allow the process of forgiveness to begin its work in me, so I do not permanently carry the pain of the hurt inside me. In forgiving another, I grieve the loss. I heal. In doing so, the hurt is prevented from growing into bitterness. I give the gift of forgiveness to myself.

The next thing we do after we choose forgiveness is to stand tall. Sometimes despite our best efforts and intentions, a conflict cannot be resolved. There are times when we can stay in the relationship and simply agree to disagree. There are other times when an unresolvable conflict forces someone to walk away.

I have experienced both outcomes on my journey. Most of my earlier experiences with conflict were never resolved well – how could they have been? I was too frantically trying to avoid the conflict or accommodate someone else's criticism or judgment. As I began to heal and grow, I began to experience myself differently, which transformed the way I experienced conflict. I no longer had to avoid conflict or abandon myself to get rid of the adversity. I could face the conflict head-on, and walk through with my head held high – such a miraculous accomplishment for me.

Not everyone thought this was such a miraculous accomplishment. Some friends liked the *old* me. They had lived with the *old* me for so long, they didn't know what to do with the *new* me. While some friends gave me the space and freedom to grow, and chose to continue walking with me, others chose not to.

While painful, I could never force a loved one to walk with me, and, in my heart, I could never turn back from my journey. I chose healing then. I choose healing today. I choose forgiveness. I choose blessing. I choose peace. How much more I cherish those relationships God *has* given me!

If we have walked through conflict well and done our best to engage collaboratively in conflict resolution, there is no need to carry guilt or shame with us. We must return to the place where we know who we are – our belovedness, our identity, our strengths and weaknesses, our beliefs and values, as well as our passions and purpose – and trust that in this season of our journey, we have experienced one more opportunity for healing and growth. The journey lasts a lifetime and even if we don't get everything right the first time around, chances are high there will be more opportunities down the road.

Stepping Stones

- As you look at the list of conflict styles, what style or styles do you tend to use? How have these styles historically worked for you in your relationships?

- Did you see any of your conflict styles used in your home growing up? Describe situations you can remember these styles at work in your family of origin.

- Can you easily remain calm when faced with conflict? If not, begin to identify specific steps you could take that would help you to calm yourself. (i.e., deep breathing exercises, prayer, guided imagery)

- Do you create an environment of compassion and cooperation in working through conflict? If not, describe how you can begin to cultivate these qualities in your relationships. How would you feel seeing the problem from someone else's perspective? How would you feel seeing your loved one and yourself on the same team?

- In preparing for a conversation, on a sheet of paper, write down the problem as you define the situation. Underneath the problem, write your specific thoughts and feelings about the problem. Practice speaking your understanding of the problem as well as your thoughts and feelings about the problem.

- Write down your defined goal. What would you like to accomplish that would allow you to feel a conflict had been successfully resolved? If you haven't done this, I encourage you to take some time to explore the answers to these questions.

- As you work through conflict and define a shared goal, is there common ground that would help you get closer to your mutual goal? Are there ways you could share power?

- How open are you to accountability? Do you have difficulty hearing someone share a problem they have with you? Write down your initial feelings and reactions to a loved one's complaint. Do you become defensive, do you deflect, stonewall, or shut-down? Do you play the victim or martyr? Explore what needs to happen for you to become more open to accountability.

- Can you recall a situation where you have appropriately owned responsibility for a problem, repented, asked for forgiveness, and made amends? If so, how did you feel afterward? What impact did your apology have on your relationship? If not, what has prevented you? Can you think of any situations where you need to own responsibility? Could you go back today and own responsibility for a situation and work through the forgiveness and amends process?

- If a loved one has never been able to own responsibility for an offense, begin today to write a letter of forgiveness to them. This letter is not meant to be sent to them; the exercise is meant to give yourself the gift of healing. Without dismissing what was done or the emotional impact you have experienced, begin to write words of forgiveness and healing to them. Pray blessing over them. In freeing them for the offense, you will, in fact, be freeing yourself.

Chapter Seventeen

CHECKING IN – THE RELATIONSHIP JOURNEY

No journey carries one far unless, as it extends into the world around us, it goes an equal distance into the world within.[48]

—Lillian Smith

Kevin and Stacy

As we near the end of our journey, we realize we have learned and applied some amazing principles for health in our relationships. Before we leave, though, we need to check in one last time with our case studies to see the progress they have made on their journeys toward peace.

---

48 Lillian Smith, http://www.iwise.com/1I2ks.

Kevin and Stacy came in, as you remember, to deal with reported communication problems. Both of them were in different places spiritually, and both had different childhood experiences that influenced how they felt about themselves and others. Kevin had never learned to be connected with himself or his emotions in a healthy way, and Stacy had never grieved the loss of her mother.

In their relationship, the combination of Kevin's passivity and resentment along with Stacy's criticism, anger, and control continued to erode any qualities of safety, openness, respect, or compassion in their relationship. Because they had never learned to connect with their thoughts and feelings, they could not share them in a healthy, respectful way. Thus, they had enormous expectations for each other that when unmet, left each feeling empty and alone. As a result, they could never successfully resolve a conflict, and they rarely ever felt like they were on the same team. The truth is, they were growing farther apart every day. They were doing what they knew to do, but things weren't getting better.

The individual work Kevin has been practicing is starting to pay off more and more. As he developed his emotional vocabulary, he felt more capable of speaking his emotions rather than acting them out. This substantially increased his confidence in his ability to take care of himself emotionally and to keep himself safe. He no longer needed Stacy to do that job for him.

Because he felt safer, he found it easier to more frequently remain calm, connected, and centered. He had begun to feel what maintaining a constant internal dialog felt like – to talk himself through his emotions, to talk himself down from many emotional ledges, and to strengthen his center of gravity.

Stacy, meanwhile, was learning how to open the door to emotions other than anger. In giving herself the gift of grieving, she was freed from the anchor of depression and anxiety that had weighed her down for so long. She connected with herself and God in a way that transformed her need for control. In knowing her identity, she could calm herself and trust that she would be okay. She could connect with her emotions and not fearfully run away from them.

Both Kevin and Stacy were learning how to own responsibility for themselves and to care for themselves well. Though there were challenges, they described feeling more calm, as well as more present with each other. Instead of having to use defense mechanisms to keep themselves safe, they could lean in and experience the other without fearing that their safety was in jeopardy. They learned more about each other, because in needing less from the other, they could open themselves up to listening – really listening to each other.

They became each other's biggest supporters as they both pursued healing and growth on their individual journeys. Kevin was not angry or resentful about Stacy's long study hours in Bible school. He loved seeing her grow. He welcomed the excitement in her eyes after a day of school. They could talk for hours about things they were learning. They invested themselves in serving at their local church. They even opened their home to a small group Bible study.

Stacy was enjoying the differences she was experiencing in Kevin. She was surprised to see him turn down so much overtime so he could spend time with her and the children. That was something he had never done before. She also loved seeing him grow in his role as a teacher in the men's ministry. Though serving in the church wasn't anything she had ever dreamed, that he was doing so was more exciting than she could imagine. She foundthat both her respect and admiration for him grew immensely.

A sense of ease and freedom gradually emerged between the two of them, and I could feel them both beginning to relax with each other. They became much more accepting of each other's differences. In session, Kevin even applauded Stacy's methodical approach to their finances as a balance and complement to his more casual, easygoing attitude about money. He no longer found their differences to be a threat, he could respect and celebrate them, understanding that both perspectives had inherent value.

They both described feeling increasingly confident they could collaborate to work through whatever differences they had to create a successful resolution. Conflict, they discovered, wasn't a bad word. To conceptualize conflict as both natural and normal was something revolutionary to them. Stacy indicated in one session that, "If conflict isn't a war to be won, then maybe I don't need all of the weapons I've been carrying around." Indeed, perhaps she doesn't.

Kevin found owning his thoughts and feelings about issues challenging. His natural tendency was always to avoid conflict and accommodate Stacy's wishes on whatever they were discussing. As we pushed in session for Kevin to practice speaking and owning his thoughts and feelings without abandoning himself, forging a collaboration where they could be on the same team was easier. That was, from what he described, what he had wanted all along–to be a team together, the two of them.

Once they experienced what being a team felt like, their relationship began to blossom in many beautiful ways. They would often reach over in the session and lovingly hold the other's hand. They were exploring new activities together and had even signed up for ballroom dancing lessons. There was a warmth and playfulness between them. They were fast becoming a couple at peace.

Jack

When we last checked in with Jack, he was slowly yet steadily healing past wounds from his childhood and building a strong foundation in his relationships with God and himself. Remarkably, the depression that had once led to a suicide attempt and subsequent hospitalization had been a turning point for Jack.

Though his journey had been tremendously challenging, the work had also been a gift. Jack was not the same person; he was proud of that. He felt stronger than he had ever felt before. He felt confident that even in difficult situations, he could walk through them well and keep himself safe. More than anything, he described feeling like a whole person. "My spiritual self and my emotional self are one now, and I don't feel conflicted or tormented anymore," he examined. "I don't need to be perfect. I don't need to beat myself up all the time. For once in my life I can embrace God's unconditional love for me as well as give that kind of love to myself. To be honest, I don't think I ever felt love before. Now I can't imagine living without it."

His relationships naturally began to evolve along the way. As his sense of self grew stronger, he didn't have to be as afraid of everything around him like he had been as a child with his mom. He became disciplined with deep breathing, guided imagery, and muscle relaxation, all of which helped him remain grounded and centered.

After he learned how to connect with his thoughts and feelings, speaking them to others around him became easier. When hidaughters would ask for money, he wasn't trapped by his need for acceptance or approval. He could lovingly and respectfully say no to them. In doing this, he found he had much more energy available to encourage them toward discovering their own solutions. Only now, he knew he didn't have to *be* the solution.

There was something powerful in learning to recognize and respect the fence around his own backyard, as well as the fences around other's backyards. In every situation, he began to ask himself, "Is this something that belongs in my backyard or is this something that belongs in somebody else's backyard?" Answering the question empowered him to determine the appropriate ownership of the problem, as well as the solution.

His daughters didn't respond well to his new approach. In fact, they were quite angry with him. They accused him of abandoning them. They blamed him for the problems in their lives. They even tried using their children as pawns to get what they wanted out of him. If dad didn't give them money, they would refuse to allow him to see his grandchildren. If dad wouldn't buy them food or clothes, or declined to fix the car they wrecked while out partying, they would simply disappear for months at a time.

Jack was prepared. He didn't need their approval so badly anymore. Neither did he need to rescue them in order to feel he was a good parent. He stood calmly and lovingly on his unshakable foundation with God and refused to be moved. He trusted God to work in his children's lives. He freed them to be with him or not be with him. Yes, he felt heartbroken at times, but he allowed God to be the source of his healing, not his daughters.

Over time, they have been coming around more. They still are not living life in a way Jack would want, but they've stopped asking for money. His youngest daughter finally got a job and has been working for about six months now. They are beginning to ask questions about God. Plus, he gets to see his grandchildren every Sunday when he takes them to church.

Things have become much freer than ever before. In session one day, he shared he had met someone at work. Though they had worked together for some time, he had never really even noticed her. He had historically always been attracted to dominant women like his mother. Shelly was not dominant. She was quiet, yet always dependable. She didn't force her opinion on others, but was ready to share if asked. While working on a project together, Jack began to notice her differently than he had before. She had a beautiful smile that exuded a depth of peace and warmth.

They have been dating exclusively for eight months. They both have adult children from previous marriages. They have had their fair share of conflict through which to work. Blended families are never easy, but with both of them committed to a healthy relationship with God and each other, they have been able to collaborate to find satisfying solutions for the issues they face. What's more, they have been able to face the issues together.

Debra

At last check-in, Debra, forty-eight years old, was battling an addiction to alcohol. As in many families, alcohol abuse/addiction is often passed from one generation to another. Debra's family was no exception. Watching her father as a child, Debra, too, learned to rely on alcohol as a way of dealing with years of pain, rejection, and loneliness. Alcohol was what she knew.

During therapy, Debra began to find other ways to deal with the pain of her past. She was able to grieve much of the trauma associated with her childhood and find healing in her relationship with God and herself. For the first time, she learned how to check into her emotions rather than to check out of them with alcohol.

One of the greatest skills Debra learned was how to calm herself. In the past, a person or situation could trigger her, taking her mind and her body to a state of heightened anxiety and distress. Once this *fight-or-flight* response kicked in, aggression was her default defense mechanism. Anger was one of the only ways in which Debra learned how to make herself safe.

Learning how to calm herself was no easy task. Being calm in uncomfortable situations went against everything she instinctively knew. The more she engaged in solitude, deep-breathing, and even Pilates exercises, the more she learned how to calm her aggression response so she did not get triggered as often or as intensely.

Becoming calmer had a positive impact on her relationships because there was much less drama. The more she grew a strong, calm center, the more she could stay connected with her thoughts and feelings. She no longer had to act out her emotions, but she could name them and speak them instead. Over time, she also discovered she had more emotions than anger. She could name fear, sadness, and even joy.

Boundaries were also a new concept for Debra. She had always understood her boundaries. She had always been proud of the fact she didn't take anything from anybody. She had determined early on she wasn't going to be anyone's doormat. She didn't just have a fence around her back-yard—she had a concrete wall. The interesting thing was as Debra learned to feel more safe with herself, she no longer needed such a mighty wall to keep her safe. She could allow others in and enjoy relationship with them without feeling vulnerable or fragile.

What she struggled with most was understanding other's boundaries. Since she had almost always been in survival mode, she had truly never considered another person's perspectives or needs. She felt as if a lightning bolt struck her when she realized other people had their own thoughts, feelings, and legitimate boundary needs. Relationship wasn't just about her.

Historically, if someone drew a boundary with Debra, she felt angry, resentful, and betrayed. She experienced their boundary as either trying to control her or as a slight against her. Certainly someone else's boundary couldn't mean any-thing positive — or could it?

What her journey thus far had allowed her to see was her instincts were honest, if not healthy responses, to a broken and unhealthy world around her growing up. Debra now had the chance to do something entirely different.

She began to see the boundaries that Tom, her new hus-band, was establishing were not meant to harm or inflict pain on her. They were meant to keep himself safe in their relationship. Tom's boundaries were meant to free him, but they were also meant to free her.

There were things he simply could not do for her. They weren't his job. By drawing a boundary, he freed Debra to look inside herself to see how she and God might be able to fill her physical or emotional needs. Finally, she could see what healthy boundaries looked like in a healthy rela-tionship, and respect another individual's refusals without feeling punished by them.

Perhaps the greatest transformation came as Debra developed healthy conflict-resolution skills. Historically, she believed, this had been her greatest strength. She was always ready for battle. She knew how to win.

Transitioning from a *kill or be killed* mentality to one where there is the possibility of having two winners was difficult, to say the least. Debra didn't back down from the challenge, though. The gains she had made on her journey thus far had felt so good, she knew she could not turn back.

She worked both in session and out of session on calming herself when her fight-or-flight response was triggered. That was her first task. Debra wouldn't be able to collaborate on anything if she was in the midst of a diffuse physiological stress state because, as we learned earlier, cognitive processing becomes flooded with emotion, and we cannot think clearly, if at all, once aroused.

As Debra strengthened her ability to stay calm, connected, and centered, she was able to think more clearly and remain in a quiet discussion rather than escalate into a fight. More than a few times, she had to take a break and go for a walk to calm herself, but she was able to resume the discussion and see the situation through to the end.

The goal of conflict had to be altered as well. Where Debra once saw the goal of conflict as winning, she grew to view the goal as successfully collaborating. She developed the capacity to hear another individual's perspective. She learned how to determine not how she could win in the conflict, but how they could both win in the conflict.

Even accepting at times there is no resolution for a conflict was challenging for Debra. She had never liked loose ends. In understanding the inherent differences between two people in a relationship, she grew to accept there were some things she and her husband would never agree on. Instead, she began to focus on creating a safe place where they could occasionally dialog and respectfully disagree.

This was especially important in their decision about whether or not to have children. Though Tom had always wanted children, Debra never had. She had always been adamant that she had been a parent to her siblings growing up and she had no intention of parenting again. That phase of her life was over.

Even as she healed and grew, her perspective did not change. This was an issue between them that was not a resolvable one, at least for now. They knew they loved each other. That they believed they were supposed to be married to one another was never in dispute. What Debra learned to focus on was not how to change her husband's mind about children, but rather how to maintain a safe, open discussion about having children.

Two years after we ended our therapy, I received a phone call from Debra. She wanted to share with me she had come to decide she was ready to have a child. Not only was she ready, she and her husband were in the middle of adopting a four-year-old special-needs child.

She was ecstatic. The longer she had cultivated Emotional Abundance into her life and relationships, the more open she became to different possibilities, the more peace she experienced. What once seemed like an impossibility had gradually become an exciting reality.

Though their backgrounds were different, though their issues were different, the one commonality among Kevin and Stacy, Jack, and Debra is their pursuit of peace. What they each learned and experienced is the process of cultivating EA into their lives, from the roots up.

Because their tree of Emotional Abundance had been planted correctly and their roots had established a solid foundation of peace in their relationship with God, that foundation created a perfect environment for peace to thrive within themselves in their core. As always occurs, peace begets more peace, flowing out to the limbs and leaves, bringing forth much fruit in all of their lives and relationships.

Life didn't become *perfect* for them. Each of the people in our case studies learned new ways of dealing with life that allowed them to experience peace in the middle of the struggles and storms that life brings. Life doesn't change—we change.

Life is not a destination—life is a journey that we are just beginning. Indeed, life is a journey where the process of healing, learning, and growing should never end. I am excited for the road that lies ahead for each of us. Press inward and onward. Our reward is the utterly satisfying state of peace—*Peace I leave with you; my peace I give you. I do not give to you as the world gives. Do not let your hearts be troubled and do not be afraid.* (John 14:27 NIV)

About the Author

First and foremost, Lisa Murray is a passionate follower of Jesus Christ. A former member of the Women of Faith worship team, Lisa worships today through her writing, encouraging readers with an authenticity and warmth that inspires hope for those who are travelling on their own journeys, struggling to find a place to rest, desperate to experience a peace that will endure. Having walked through her own struggles with anxiety, despair, and perfectionism, Lisa enjoys helping others as they explore and discover spiritual and emotional healing in their lives and relationships.

Lisa is a Licensed Marriage and Family Therapist, with an undergraduate degree from Vanderbilt University, as well as a graduate degree from Trevecca University.

In 2007, Lisa founded the Counseling and Family Ministries at Grace Chapel in Leipers Fork, TN, where she not only works to help individuals, couples, and families, deal with the complexities and challenges of life and relationships, she also treats a full spectrum of mental health issues.

A journey borne from her personal experiences, *"Peace for a Lifetime"* compassionately guides readers on their journey from brokenness and despair to wholeness, abundance and ultimately – peace! Lisa writes Blog posts at www. lisamurrayonline.com. You can connect with her on Facebook at Lisa Murray or Twitter @_Lisa_Murray.

At the end of the day, Lisa is just a Southern girl who loves beautiful things, whether it is the beauty of words found in a deeply moving story, the beauty of a meal cooked with love, the beauty of a cup of coffee with a friend, or the beauty seen in far away landscapes and cultures. She has fallen passionately in love with the journey and believes it is among the most beautiful gifts to embrace and celebrate. While she grew up in the Florida sunshine, Lisa and her husband Mark live just outside of Nashville in Franklin, TN.

48607641R00142

Made in the USA
Charleston, SC
08 November 2015